T0167022

Two Guys Read Jane Austen

Steve Chandler and Terrence N. Hill

Authors of *Two Guys Read Moby-Dick* and *Two Guys Read the Obituaries*

Robert D. Reed Publishers   ●   Bandon, OR

Robert D. Reed Publishers
P.O. Box 1992
Bandon, OR 97411
Phone: 541-347-9882 • Fax: -9883
E-mail: 4bobreed@msn.com
web site: www.rdrpublishers.com

Editor: **Kathy Chandler**
Cover Designer: **Cleone Lyvonne**
Cover Photographer: **"Retro Wallpaper"**
                     © Jon Helgason from dreamstime.com
Authors' Photographer: **Kathy Eimers**
Typesetter: **Barbara Kruger**

ISBN: 978-1-934759-17-2

Library of Congress Control Number 2008933641

Manufactured, typeset and printed in the United States of America

Dedication

To Steve

(I know this isn't normal – dedicating the book to one of the authors. But, totally aside from his being my best friend for more than 50 years, I'd like to acknowledge publicly Steve's role as the driving force behind these books that have afforded me so very much pleasure in the making. *TNH*)

Introduction

What guy really wants to read Jane Austen?

Terry Hill is a man who knows how to read and knows how to write. I mean this in the most artistic, professional sense. I've known him for over 50 years and this is the third book I've written with him. (The other two are *Two Guys Read Moby-Dick* and *Two Guys Read the Obituaries* ... that last one was written with a panicky speed so that we wouldn't be cited in our own book.)

Terrence N. Hill is the author of the Playhouse-on-the-Green award-winning play, "Hamlet – the Sequel." (In that play, by the way, the lead character's name is Terry Hill. A coincidence that gives me goose bumps every time I think about it.)

When we were in high school Terry and I double-dated. As boys we played on sports teams together. He was at shortstop, while I played third. Our teams were difficult for other teams to beat. We once sang as a folk duo in a bar. We've been whaling, delivered newspapers together, given toasts at each other's weddings and now it has come to this ... reading Jane Austen. What was there left to do?

And for me, I'd made it through sixty some years without reading Austen at all and so I thought I was pretty much home free. What guy, really, wants to read Jane Austen?

I mean, *Moby-Dick* was one thing. A manly adventure, containing no women at all! Reading and writing about the tall tale of courage and madness on the high seas would be fun – and indeed it was. *Two Guys Read Moby-Dick* got such a surprisingly enthusiastic response that we decided to do more books this way. The fun was just beginning.

Then came death. Or, rather, the obituaries. Terry was an avid obituary reader, often clipping them and sending them to me over the years, especially when the deceased was someone from the world of music, sports or literature. These have been shared interests of ours since we first became friends in 1955. For the obits book we read the obituaries every day for a year and commented on them. We explored the meaning of life and death ... in our way. Deep stuff, as you can imagine.

And now our third book, the most dangerous territory yet, the world of Jane Austen. Do real men really read Jane Austen? We were fearless in the face of that question.

Even though I had a degree in English, I somehow managed to navigate through a lot of authors in college without reading Jane. No I was not a misogynist. Don't lump me in with them. I wasn't a guy like Pat Robertson who once said, "The key in terms of mental ability is chess. There's never been a woman Grand Master chess player. Once you get one, then I'll buy some of the feminism." (I would hand that lip-moving, mouth-breathing charlatan cathode-ray minister a copy of Emily Dickinson so he would indeed be in the presence of a true chess master. But I get ahead of myself.)

Before this assignment – reading *Pride and Prejudice* and *Mansfield Park* – my only exposure to Jane Austen had been through film. There were so many good movies based on her books, movies like *Sense and Sensibility* and the Colin Firth *Pride and Prejudice* of the BBC and even the funny movie *Clueless* which was based on Jane Austen's book, *Emma*. Such good movies! But that was enough Jane for me. I had no desire whatsoever to read what I assumed was chick lit that had simply translated entertainingly into chick flicks.

So when Terry's wife Miranda and my wife Kathy both suggested that Jane Austen be the subject of our next book I thought it would be a hilarious romp of mockery. Like Terry and me sitting on the couch with beer and chips yelling funny comments at the stupid love scenes before switching back to the Michigan-Ohio State game. I was locked and loaded, ready to fire even more ridicule than he and I fired at *Moby-Dick*.

So now we have two grown men in their early sixties (sixty is the new thirty, remember) reading Jane Austen together! It sounds like something an army psychological warfare unit would turn to if waterboarding were outlawed. As a way to break a man. Break him down and surrender his manhood forever.

In a recent writer's workshop delivered in Mexico, Terry quoted J.D. Salinger who said only two questions should be asked of a writer after he'd written something – "Were most of your stars out? Were you busy writing your heart out?"

Those are questions Jane Austen would have to answer for me. And in the book that follows you'll witness the rather amusing spectacle of my encountering something I certainly had not expected.

Steve Chandler – April, 2008

24 September 2007 – Georgian Bay, Canada
Dear Steve,

Do you know what an angioplasty is?

It's a medical procedure, and believe me, I'd be very much in the dark about it myself if it weren't for having once worked on a medical account in advertising. (I've always made a distinct point of walking away from any health or medical discussion unless there's money in it for me. I'm going to make a very unsatisfactory old man I'm afraid.)

Angioplasty is used on patients with clogged veins (or maybe arteries, I'm not sure.) In order to open the flow of blood, the operation involves putting a tiny balloon into the vein and then inflating it to enlarge the vein and facilitate the flow. (I know this can't be, but I picture a bicycle pump being used at this point in the surgery.) It all sounds very *Fantastic Voyage*, doesn't it?

I bring up this bit of medical trivia because Miranda suspects that a similar procedure has been performed on Anne Hathaway's lips and I was hoping you and Kathy could weigh in with an opinion. We just saw Anne in the film *Becoming Jane* as part of my rigorous preparation for starting this book. The film is supposed to be based on the real circumstances of Jane Austen's life. In fact, while the circumstances may be real enough, the story is pure fantasy. Still it makes for, I thought, a fun movie.

Anne plays Jane Austen in the film. This is a bit of a casting stretch. There are only two known pictures of Jane – both amateur efforts by her sister Cassandra – and if they represent a passable likeness, then Jane was not nearly as pretty as Anne Hathaway. Nor were her lips as inflated. On the other hand, surgery had not advanced to the *Fantastic Voyage* stage in 1800 either. Still I must say I thought Anne a terrific Jane Austen.

Miranda didn't much like her, but then, in my experience, Anne Hathaway is a bit of a litmus test. If you like her, you're a man; if you don't, you're a woman. I find her perfectly beautiful in a romantic, virginal kind of way. Women find her too perfect and too perky.

This male/female divide is interesting as we approach Jane's books because so much of what drives her stories is about just that: the differences between how men and women think and feel. Which is, of course, what lured us into this venture in the first place.

The release of *Becoming Jane* is also a welcome sign for us, Steve. Have you noticed that mast on the horizon? That, my friend, is our ship coming in. Finally we have found a subject that is guaranteed to bring us John Grisham-like royalties.

We are about to cash in on the Jane Austen boom – it's all around us. *Becoming Jane* is in theaters now; a film called the *Jane Austen Book Club* launches next week; Jane is all over the web – I read an article that said one Jane Austen site draws over 10 million hits per month! And that's just one site.

Even better, given some women's foolish objection that our two previous books had too much male sports talk, the audience for that Austen website is 98% women. Believe me we're into the mother lode! And I'm ready to get to the opening chapters of *Pride and Prejudice* right now.

terry.

27 September 2007 – Gilbert, Arizona
dear terry,

I know this book is different. When I told our friend Dick Schwarze, an athlete, a hunter, a fisherman, that our third book would be about Jane Austen, he gave me a "please tell me you're kidding" type of response.

I think men have a hard time with women authors. Anthony Burgess once wrote that women put all their creative magic into creating children and therefore couldn't have much left over to write with. In his biography Burgess wrote about how his drunken wife used to read all the cheap romance novels "and Jane Austen" so he could never separate Jane from the cheap and shallow. He called Jane Austen "that scribbling spinster."

Mark Twain said, "Jane Austen? Why I go so far as to say that any library is a good library that does not contain a volume by Jane Austen. Even if it contains no other book."

In his wonderful song "Highlands," Bob Dylan is being waited on in a cafe by an intriguing waitress who accuses him of not reading women authors.

Then she says,"You don't read women authors do ya?"
at least that's what I think I hear her say.
Well, I said, "How would you know and what would it matter anyway?"
Well she says, "You just don't seem like you do." I said, "You're way wrong."
She says "Which ones have you read then?" I say, "I've read Erica Jong."

The fun I had reading the first 11 chapters of *Pride and Prejudice* while on vacation last week in Boston and Cape Cod had me admiring Jane more than I expected. I'd read a lot ABOUT her writing, and some samples here and there, but never a book start to finish like this.

Philip Roth in a recent interview said he was reading Hemingway's *The Sun Also Rises* as part of his final farewell to the masters. He's reading all the great books one last time. Farewell? Roth was born in 1933, which makes him 75. His generation thinks that's old. Time to say farewell.

But do we? I think not. You said you were going to make a very unsatisfactory old man. And you put that in the future. Thank you. We are barely in our sixties. 60 *is* the new 30. No farewell reading tours for me. Not yet, anyway.

You asked that Kathy and I weigh in on the possibility of plastic surgery for Anne Hathaway in *Becoming Jane*. We saw the movie yesterday, and thought it a wonderfully entertaining movie. However, Kathy and I both voted "no" on Hathaway's inflated lip surgery. She just has those lips. She is too young to have had the inflations. Not that we are naive about this subject. We follow the stars. We note the worst plastic surgeries, such as those performed on Priscilla Presley and Nancy Sinatra. For me, the most disappointing angioLIPplasty was done on Meg Ryan. Once America's sweetheart, she somehow thought she was getting old and had the work done on her lips and no longer looks like anyone's sweetheart. If any sweet feelings occur when looking at her today it's because she reminds us of the little yellow duck we used to float in the bathtub when we were children.

I'm beginning to think Jane Austen would never have done this procedure. She was not needy in spirit. She even turned down a suitor or two in her lifetime. By her own choice. So maybe she was not the bitter "spinster" Burgess jealously said she was. There seems to have been nothing artificial or inflated about her.
Steve

28 September 2007 – Georgian Bay, Canada (Pride & Prejudice: chapters 1-11)
Steve,

That famous first sentence: "It is a truth universally acknowledged that a single man in possession of a good fortune must be in want of a wife." It makes me smile once again.

It's interesting, I think, that with the subject of our first book (*Moby-Dick*) and now with *Pride and Prejudice* we have perhaps the two most famous first lines in all of English fiction. But when I look now at "Call me Ishmael." I wonder what made it so famous. It seems kind of neutral to me. And it hardly sets up the book. I suppose it sets up the narrator, but to what end? Frankly I never felt the need to call him Ishmael despite his invitation.

Austen's first line, on the other hand, seems the perfectly-dealt opening card. Now I know that I have the advantage of you here. After all, I've read *P&P* three times in my life, while you are virtually a Jane Austen virgin. But it strikes me, reading the sentence this time, how brilliantly it sets up the whole novel and manages our expectations. In the first place the subject of the sentence – the pursuit of husbands – is what the next 400 pages are all about. But secondly, it's amusing and therefore, not inaccurately, promises amusement in addition to a story.

Again I fall in love with Jane and I envy you the chance to discover her for the first time.

More evidence that we've hit the big time by taking on Jane Austen:

I recently visited a college fraternity brother of mine named Dick Johnson. His wife, in honor of my visit I suppose, had just read and liked (or at least said nice things about) *Two Guys Read the Obituaries*. She asked me what we were working on now and I told her about this project. She looked at me with steely eyes for a moment before saying, "You better be kind to Darcy." There was a definite threat in her voice, and believe me, she wasn't kidding.

I don't know about your experience, but in the past when I told anyone that I was working on a book about reading *Moby-Dick* or reading obituaries, the response was usually something like, "I've just taken up lawn bowling myself," or "Do you think flossing really works?"

Let's face it, as great a book as *Two Guys Read Moby-Dick* is, when it comes to Melville, most people can pretty much take him or leave him (most opting for the latter.) That ain't the case with Jane Austen: people are passionate about her. I say "people" but I guess I mean "women." Jane's got more adoring female fans than Brad Pitt, and my guess is they're more intelligent too.

And as Bridget Johnson demonstrates, they're not just fans of Jane's, they also have deep attachments to her characters. A small misstep in a sentence about Darcy on our part and death threats may result.

Still I urge courage. We must cast a cold eye on Darcy and let the chips fall where they may.

The original title of *Pride and Prejudice*, as you may have noticed in the movie *Becoming Jane*, was *First Impressions*. Now that we've read the first eleven chapters, I suggest we've had long enough to form our "first impressions" of the characters, so here are a few of mine:

Elizabeth is, as Jane intended her to be, my favorite. I've always had a weakness for a girl with a bit of a mouth on her and, by Regency standards, she definitely qualifies. She's witty, bright, sensible and seems to have very little in the way of vanity.

Likewise her sister Jane, who despite her much-talked-about beauty, also seems to be sensible and without vanity.

This brings up the question of how these girls turned out so well growing up under the influence of their embarrassing mother. I totally share Miss Bingley's opinion of Mrs. Bennet.

Mr. Bingley seems an amiable nonentity, while Darcy is clearly (sorry, Bridget) a self-important prig. As you no doubt know, Steve, Darcy goes through a transformation during the novel and by the end we're all supposed to admire his wonderful qualities. Well, it may work on women, but even at the end, underneath his shiny veneer, I suspect he still has the makings of a self-important prig.

I'm at a cottage on Georgian Bay about two hours north of Toronto, and among the books that crowd the bookshelves I found an issue of *South Shore*, the literary journal you used to edit years ago. I picked it up yesterday just after receiving your e-mail and found a short essay on women writers written by my father. In it he talks about *Fear of Flying* and Erica Jong.

As you once told me, there are no coincidences.

t.

29 September 2007 – Gilbert, Arizona
Ter,

I hate to say it, but this is just pure fun reading this book.

Could I have read this and enjoyed it as a teenager? Definitely not.

For a host of reasons, but mainly because of my feelings about women back then. I believe many men form their impressions of women early in life from their mothers. Unfortunately for me (and her) my relationship with my own mother was a very negative one because of her drinking.

As a younger boy I didn't know that she would start drinking early in the day. So it just looked to me like she was going insane, getting sloppier and more stupid as the day progressed. Subconsciously, I formed an impression of women as sloppy, shallow and astonishingly stupid.

It was just the alcohol.

But I had a lot of unlearning to do. And once I saw that it *was* the alcohol (and some pills, too, don't forget those) that made my mother (and women to me) a caricature, I could allow myself to get to know her better and see the true beauty of her soul beneath all the poison…and she was a truly beautiful, bright person. And it didn't hurt that she spent her last few years clean, clear, free and sober.

One help in improving my perception of women was your own mother. As a boy, I spent a lot of time at your house. People thought I was the fourth Hill brother. Your own mom was a great character, a bright, funny, strong, attractive redhead who taught school and enjoyed great conversation. (Funny to note that you have written a song about your mother and I have written a song about my father.)

I think God wanted to cure me of this, too! Once I got married (after waiting until I was 35 to do so, in those days a long delay) right away I had three daughters! All of them bright and feisty and independent!

The two most interesting characters in this book, Mr. Darcy and Elizabeth Bennet, begin the story not liking each other at all. Elizabeth finds Darcy pompous; while Darcy thinks Elizabeth not even worthy of a dance. She's not as pretty as her older sister and clearly not on his social level. This last negative is brought home by Elizabeth's absurdly crass mother, always trying too overtly to get her daughters married off.

But soon Elizabeth's dark, alluring eyes, quick wit and supreme self-assurance start to ring the alarm bells in Mr. Darcy's heart. And here is where I grudgingly admit that Jane Austen is good. She knows how to use intelligence as a form of flirtation. So while we are seeing Elizabeth spar and fence verbally with Darcy, we vicariously fall for her. She is feisty, independent, courageously witty and yet possesses a deep sense of honor and propriety.

As I began reading the first eleven chapters, I was in Boston on the front end of a New England vacation Kathy and I were taking. We took a trolley tour of Boston one day and the tour guides were so entertaining and evocative in their accounts of Boston's revolutionary days and the heroic men and women who rebelled against the British in such innovative ways that I was inspired to buy David McCullough's famous biography of John Adams to read concurrently with this book. (The era is the same! Jane Austen was born in 1775.) Both books are exciting, in completely different ways.

Knowing Jane Austen's life story allows me to see a lot of her in Elizabeth Bennet. The fact that Miss Austen had to publish this book anonymously (because she was a woman, and writing novels just wasn't an acceptable activity for women back then) gives you an idea of the courage she had and the belief in her own talent.

Elizabeth Bennet is considered to be of the country, and of less social stature than Darcy and his friends. Yet she plays piano and reads widely and holds deep philosophical insights that she knows how to express fearlessly and eloquently in the company of gentlemen. She has no desire to win anyone over. So she can, as she says, enjoy pure humor and irony. She is free.

Just as John Adams and the colonists were rebelling against the British, physically and literally, so was Jane, in the character of Elizabeth Bennet, rebelling against the stuffy Britain of the 18th Century ... a Britain in which women were only empowered by marrying men, because of the societal and cultural restrictions that caused so many problems of inheritance, courtship, morals, and arranged marriages. Jane Austen (through Elizabeth) is a witty, rebellious voice for intelligence and passion in the face of those stuffy British strictures. I love this. I love a woman (or a man, for that matter) who has no need to win anyone over.

My favorite author of books on psychology and spirituality is Byron Katie, who says, "If I had one prayer it would be God spare me from the desire for love, approval, or appreciation. Amen."

Steve.

30 sept 08 – Georgian Bay, Ontario, Canada
steve.

As a way of keeping me on my toes and making sure I don't slip away to the old folks' home prematurely, I've encouraged Miranda to be a keen observer of the aging process. Characteristically, she's taken her assignment seriously. As a result of her rigorous studies, she has identified what she calls The Four Stages of Age:

The first telltale sign of aging, she found, is that one starts reading the Op-Ed page in the newspaper. Though I have never been tempted by the editorial page myself, I suspect she is right. Because lately I've noted that a lot of my friends, now that they are older, have started sending me the occasional editorial.

The next stage, Miranda tells me, is marked by a fascination with nature shows. When you bump into a friend at a bar and he opens the conversation by mentioning that he just saw a particularly good show on prairie dogs last evening, you know he's slipped into this second stage. Sudden knowledge of the Galapagos Islands is also clear evidence. I believe the entire *March of the Penguins* phenomenon can be explained by the coincident aging of the Baby Boomers.

The third stage is recognizable by a newfound interest in reading biographies. Here I would gently take notice of your recent reading of the John Adams biography. Miranda tells me that this is *not necessarily* cause for panic.

If, however, you tell me that you've now taken up writing letters to the editor, then there would be no doubt but that you've moved into the fourth stage. Your next move should be to google "caskets."

t.

1 October 2007 – Gilbert, Arizona
Ter,

The nation state of Israel is celebrating its 60th birthday soon. A possible calling card for me "OLDER THAN ISRAEL."

s.

2 Oct 2007 – Georgian Bay, Canada
Steve,

You know I just took a look at Dad's essay in that long-ago *South Shore* I found up here at the cottage and I note he had pretty good things to say about *Fear of Flying*.

"It's not bad," he wrote. "Ms. Jong is a writer. I treasure the book for a single line: 'God has punished the Germans for being such pigs by making them look like pigs.'"

Which *is* a pretty funny line, no matter how un-PC it might be. Maybe I should read *Fear of Flying*.

t.

5 October 2007 – Gilbert, Arizona

dear terry,

Funny but wrong. Some of the most beautiful people I have known have been Germans. Alexandra Maria Lara. Maria Schell. Romy Schneider. Marlene Dietrich. I lived in Berlin for over a year, and I was constantly amazed at how beautiful the Germans were. Germans I know today are quite good looking.

I received in the mail today some interesting articles from you about weight loss. It's a theme we began together in *Two Guys Read Moby-Dick* when you introduced your calorie-star-game system. It's a great system. How do I know? I am now 16 pounds lighter than I was when we wrote that book.

Thank you.

These days weight is getting scary in America. On both ends of the scale. On one end you see the rampant obesity epidemic (especially in airports, or even more dramatic, at a state fair.)

On the other end you see actresses like Angelina Jolie, Cate Blanchett and Hilary Swank starving themselves so thin that they look skeletal and cadaverous, which is not really all that attractive, so what could they be thinking? [*I'm not sure Cate should have been included in Steve's list of anorexstars. I didn't think so at the time and I got support for this view when five months later she showed up at the Oscars very pregnant and looking well-fed. TNH.*]

Now take Jane Austen's point of view. In *P&P*, when she introduces Elizabeth's 15-year-old young sister Lydia, she admiringly calls her "stout." Which in those days meant flush with radiant flesh. Not obese. But not skeletal either. A full, sexy figure. Jane Austen didn't use the word "sexy" for Lydia; she said instead that Lydia was a "stout, well-grown girl of fifteen, with a fine complexion … and high animal spirits."

We know what that means. She flirts with soldiers. She's an animal. In the best sense. Hardly in search of a diet or a plastic surgeon.

The articles you sent on weight loss said that one's caloric restriction (for weight loss) should take into account whether one exercises. I know you walk each day. I go to our health club about four days a week and walk the others. And I'm increasing this routine. I also sing every day for an hour. Don't laugh. It is said to add 15 years to your life to do that! Look what happened to Pavorotti when he stopped singing. One should never stop singing.

The women in *Pride and Prejudice* all speak French and Italian and play musical instruments and do elaborate crafts, etc. That was what they did in that era in that community in England. Today if a woman speaks three languages, plays piano and does a craft we call her some sort of rare multifaceted genius.

I think the obesity epidemic comes from not playing the piano. It comes from watching and listening instead of participating. (I know that theory is correct when I apply it to myself and any weight I gain.) They actually have TV shows now called "reality shows." I know you don't watch much TV, Terry, so you'll just have to take my word for this. There really are "reality" shows. I think the reality shows are there so that viewers don't have to engage real reality. They can just watch others engage in it.

Are we perhaps over-saturating ourselves with pleasure and entertainment? Being obsessive spectators? Not writing plays but rather watching them. Not dancing but watching "Dancing with the Stars." Not playing sports but watching them. Not playing music but rather listening to it all day. Not wrestling a real criminal to the ground, but playing "Grand Theft Auto" or "Halo II" instead.

Reading Jane Austen might change all that for me. It is starting to make me excited about writing again. I read an article in *USA Today* about the movie *Becoming Jane* and the star, Anne Hathaway, was asked why she thought there are so many movies and books about Jane Austen these days. She said, "I think there's an excellence to Jane Austen that people crave. Right now, I think it's fair to say that mediocrity is being celebrated, and Austen will never stop being excellent. So it's very reassuring."

s.

16 October – New York City
Steve,

I'm back in New York after two months on the road around the Great Lakes. We actually laid eyes on four of the five Great ones on the trip. Miranda called it the Terry Hill Reunion Tour because of all the dinners, lunches, get-togethers etc. we had with friends, family and acquaintances of mine.

I spent a good part of the time each day explaining to Miranda the backgrounds and connections to me of the people we'd be meeting that night. (Our dinner with you and Kathy in Detroit in August was about the only event not requiring an extensive briefing.)

It was like a catalog of characters – major and minor – in some novel of my life. And, thought of that way, I couldn't help thinking what a rather aimless and – very probably – dull novel it would be.

And right there is where Jane Austen's brilliance shames me! Working with a smaller and much less worldly cast of characters she created these wonderful, wonderful novels.

On the trip back from Georgian Bay we stopped in Toronto and managed to squeeze in the new movie *The Jane Austen Book Club*. Miranda quite liked the film and I enjoyed it too, though my enjoyment was severely undermined by thinking how alternately banal and pretentious the club members' comments on Jane's novels were.

I'm afraid it reminded me too much of the kinds of pithy insights I had imagined myself springing on you in this correspondence. I do so hate being banal or pretentious, but even more, I hate the thought of being *predictably* banal or pretentious – of being pedestrian and unoriginal. I suspect this is true of all of us who presume to be serious about writing.

I take solace, however, in a thought of Sir Leslie Stephens's: "Originality does not consist in saying what no one has ever said before, but in saying exactly what you think yourself." Then again, I'm not sure I'm even capable of pulling that off. [*Stephens managed to pass his knowledge of originality on to his daughter, the writer, Virginia Woolf, who was definitely an original. TNH*]

Film has always loved Jane Austen. I am thinking not just of the recent spate of Jane-related films like *Becoming Jane* and *The Jane Book Club*, but also of all of the film versions of her six novels. According to *imdb.com* there have been 29 film versions of her books. I am counting only the films taken directly from her books. I didn't count movies like *Clueless*, that modern day version of *Emma* you mentioned earlier, or *Bridget Jones Diary*, which is, of course, the melding of *Pride and Prejudice* and Weight Watchers.

29 films! headed by nine versions of *Pride and Prejudice*. And so many of them have been really well done, like the five-hour BBC version of *P&P*.

But let me ask you – have you *ever* seen a film of a book you've read and not walked away thinking the book was better no matter how good the film was? I know it's an unfair comparison and that they are two entirely different mediums, but I can't think of a single case in my experience. So, back to the book:

Don't you just love Mr. Collins? These chapters (12-20) get us through the older Bennet sister's illness crisis, introduce the charming Wickham and further establish Lizzy's dislike of Darcy. But it is also here that Austen introduces one of her great comic characters in Mr. Collins, the ass-kissing, self-deluding buffoon of a clergyman. I'll bet that by the time you reach the end of the novel, you'll find yourself laughing every time he makes an appearance.

He reminds me of the Ted Knight character on the old "Mary Tyler Moore Show."

Of course Mr. Bennet has already taken his measure and it allows him to get off perhaps the second funniest line in the book when he tells Lizzy that as far as he's concerned she can turn down Mr. Collins's proposal of marriage, thus countermanding Mrs. Bennet's insistence.

I read the assertion once that Jane Austen is the bedrock on which all of "chick lit" and "romance" fiction rests. Without Jane, no Helen Fielding, no Danielle Steele. I'm sure there is truth in this though one suspects the quality is much higher in the founder of the thread. On the other hand, I don't think Austen ever gets proper credit for her role in the development of the comic novel. Maybe this is because the books are seen as serious literature … maybe it's because the central characters are generally principled and serious themselves … whatever the reason, I find the books always very amusing and often just laugh-aloud funny.

Some of this lies in characters like Mrs. Bennet and Mr. Collins, either of whom – with an updated wardrobe – could comfortably reside in a Wodehouse novel. But much more of it comes from Austen's ironic turn of mind and the sheer virtuosity of the writing.

I mean how perfect is that Mr. Bennet line in chapter 20?

"An unhappy alternative is before you, Elizabeth. From this day you must be a stranger to one of your parents. You mother will never see you again if you do not marry Mr. Collins, and I will never see you again if you do."

Oh yes, I called that the *second* funniest line? The *first* funniest will come much later in the book and I will not spoil it for you by leaking it now. But I will say that I was 23 and in law school when my father, who was reading *Pride and Prejudice* at the time, read the line to me. I had not read a single word of Jane Austen at the time and it was hearing the line that prompted me to read her.

terry.

17 October 2007 – Gilbert, Arizona
terry

And they say there are no true heroines today? What about Miranda for taking your Reunion Tour with you? Having to drive around all the Great Lakes to meet everyone you ever knew! I bet she never complained.

But I bet she's glad to be back on the isle of Manhattan.

I can't wait to see you there in a couple of weeks; I'll be using my day of work with a client as an excuse to be with you and Miranda again. Last time I was there you and she took me to see a great, edgy young country singer whose upcoming album was called, "Drinking With Jesus," an album of drinking songs and spirituals, many of which he sang for us that night.

Traveling is fun for me but it has its drawbacks. One time when I was in the airport baggage claim area I saw an old lady wheeling my red suitcase away and I had to chase her down. It's amazing how many suitcases look alike these days. Well it turned out it wasn't actually my suitcase, but that's beside the point. It could have been.

The point was I wanted to eliminate the anxiety associated with never knowing for sure which suitcase was mine. And because I fly about once a week, it had become important to me. I thought I had solved the problem by buying a red suitcase. But alas, no, there were red suitcases cropping up everywhere.

I noticed that some people try to solve this problem by putting little strands of yarn on their suitcases. But I would not consider that. It simply looked too feminine. This is yarn left over from my knitting? I was knitting a sweater for the poodle? No. A man must travel as a man.

So Kathy got the idea of painting my suitcase. Not the whole thing, but just a few spots. She bought a stencil set and painted various black circles and crescents on my red suitcase.

When Kathy does something, she likes to do a thorough job. She is not haphazard like I often am. She is comprehensive and complete. So by the time she was finished with my suitcase there were LOTS of circles and crescents all over my suitcase. Like in the West Side Story song, there were "suns and moons all over the place."

It is no longer difficult for me to find my suitcase in a crowd. It really stands out. As I was checking my bag yesterday morning for Vancouver, the ticket counter lady looked at it and said, "Oh my goodness, are you a magician?"

I get these kinds of questions a lot now. Yes, I am a traveling magician, a wizard with a whole suitcase of tricks. And I have to tell you that this is creating a new kind of anxiety. But good times are ahead because this suitcase appears to be broken. So I can buy a new one. I may also buy some yarn to go with it.

You're right about books being better than film. Books can do so much more. Film is restricted. In books, you can take your time and read and re-read at your own chosen speed. You can go deep into complex personal motivations. Movies live on the surface.

The reason Jane Austen is better than cheap romance novels is that there is never the shallow "hunk" factor. The whole physical element is only suggested. The true measure of her characters is their hearts and minds. All the movie versions can do – as good as some of them are – is make Darcy look like Colin Firth and Mr. Collins a portly and ugly turn-off! But that's so superficial compared to what's really repulsive about Mr. Collins. His lack of integrity. His lack of authenticity.

And because you spoke of your own life as an inferior novel, I will bring up an aspect of your life that is not. There are many aspects I can name, but this is striking … it is downright Dickensian (if not Nabokovian): When you were growing up, you had a series of crushes on various girls, and the one thing these girls all had in common was that their first names and last names began with the same letter! Tina Thren. Jennifer Jackson. Linda Long. I could go on. And I admit that those girls were certainly worthy of crushes, (for I longed for Linda myself) but some strange novel was being written with that ... maybe we could even say ... *Joycean* alliteration. In this one aspect, I think you'll have to rate your life as superior to Jane Austen's novel ... the character names in *P&P* are fairly mundane.

You mentioned our dinner in Michigan a few weeks ago. During that dinner we were all raving about how great Netflix is, and noting how little TV any of us watch any more. You then said that the only exception was sports.

I said that no, I didn't even watch baseball on TV – not even with our Arizona Diamondbacks having the best record in the National League. You were surprised. But please don't be. They were a team that was very hard to watch. Why? They could not hit the baseball. So you would sit there for three hours watching people *not* do something. It would be like going to an Eric Clapton concert and have him just sit up there on a chair and *not* play. You would not like that concert. Especially if it lasted three hours.

It's a far better use of free time to sneak off and read *Pride and Prejudice*, in which a writer actually writes.

Steve

20 October 2007 – NYC
steve.

Yes, those double-lettered ladies were amazing. I must have had alliteration in my romance hard drive. I can trace the phenomenon back as far as second grade when my main crush was Pamela Pepper. Fortunately I had mostly weaned myself off it by the time I got to high school, though vestiges of the quirk would from time to time crop up again in later life. (Could I point out here that Jane Austen's first two books are *S&S* and *P&P*?)

Well, I might have gone a bit overboard on Jane Austen. You decide:

In addition to reading a regular text of *Pride and Prejudice*, I have also bought and am reading an annotated version, which is so copiously annotated that it stretches to more than two times the length of the novel. More than 3000 footnotes! It's fabulous. But it means that, in effect, I am reading *Pride and Prejudice* twice right now.

But that's not all, I also bought two biographies of Jane Austen. First, *Becoming Jane*, on which the movie was based (sort of), and second, a compact biography by the recently deceased Canadian novelist Carol Shields who won the Pulitzer Prize for fiction back in 1995. In addition I just watched the DVD of *Mansfield Park*.

I am awash in Jane. And I can't tell you how thrilling I find it. The weather has been unseasonably wonderful here – mid-70s and sunny – and I've been taking all my Jane books to Washington Square Park and reading there, dipping first into one, then another until I resentfully have to leave for some appointment or other.

I don't want to overwhelm you with all my new knowledge of the author and the books, but I might just venture a couple of interesting bits:

1) Reading the biographies, it is clear that there is a lot of Jane Austen in Elizabeth Bennet. I refer not so much to incidents in the author's life that have been put into the novel, though there are some of these, but more to the personality and spirit of the heroine. Not surprisingly, Austen was exceedingly fond of Elizabeth. Jane wrote about Elizabeth in a letter: "I must confess I find her as delightful a creature as ever appeared in print."

2) Jane never attended school after the age of 11. After that she was entirely self-taught. In chapter 29 of *P&P*, Elizabeth describes her similar education, explaining to Lady Catherine de Bourgh that she "was always encouraged to read." And yet this unstructured education seems to have served. For though Austen never had a book published until she was 36, between the ages of 18 and 25 she wrote three

complete novels: *Elinor and Marianne*, *First Impressions* and *Susan*. All three were later published with revisions under the titles *Sense and Sensibility*, *Pride and Prejudice* and *Northanger Abbey*.

Three of the greatest novels of all time – all written by 25.

Thinking back to myself at that age. If I had had time on my hands I could well imagine having written three novels, for even then I wanted to be a writer. What I *can't* imagine, even with the most extreme revisionist memory, is that they would have been any good. Ah, but then I had the disadvantage of an education.

Now before you charge me with false modesty, let me warn you that in our home in Mexico I have concrete evidence of the quality of my writing at that age in the form of hundreds of letters written to friends (including, obviously, a lot to you.)

Reading them is like a religious experience for me. Unfortunately, the experience I have in mind is Saint Sebastian's. Every sentence is like an arrow piercing my pride, my confidence and my general impression of my writing abilities. They are unbelievably embarrassing.

When we go back down to San Miguel in January, I intend to burn them. I realize this act will upset my biographers, but hopefully they will ascribe it to some scandalous love affair I was trying to cover up rather than the simple truth of my utter lack of early talent.

terry.

26 October 2007 – Gilbert, AZ
Dear Terry,

Okay burn the teen writings … even the writings in your 20s. There is a reason, however, that you weren't close to Jane's level back then … the reason?

Sports.

Jane didn't have to follow sports the way you and I did, literally knowing by heart every single player in major league baseball and also knowing more about college and pro football and basketball etc. than most sportswriters did.

In fact, later I actually became a sportswriter. And one of the first things I observed about my fellow sportswriters was that they didn't really follow sports as obsessively as you and I did. They did not know what you and I knew. It scared me. All the long hours playing intricate self-made games with our baseball cards (those valuable cards our mothers threw away in a wild attempt to break the addiction ... also in an attempt to have us start out in life without any unfair financial advantages. If they had preserved all those cards we'd have millions of dollars today.)

So Jane had no baseball cards at age 11 when she stopped school and became an autodidact. No sports to follow. You and I also had mesmerizing junior high school girls to follow and fantasize about ... almost mythological in beauty and allure ... for if they didn't have poetic, alliterative names like Tina Thren and Jennifer Jackson, then they just had lovely names, like Rose Mormon or Leigh Young. While Jane Austen was missing all this junior high school awakening, we had our hands full.

What, we're supposed to develop as writers, too? I don't think so.

Books were all Jane had.

I think good writing requires a huge, amazing amount of reading. How else do you get the feel of how writing really happens? Since those youthful letters you wrote, you have read a great deal. I mean, look at how you just toss off a reference to Saint Sebastian like I will know who that is.

I had to go to Wikipedia. Then, of course, I vaguely remembered that Saint Sebastian was a famous martyr. His image appears in a lot of great art and literature. In her short story "Everything That Rises Must Converge" (which I read in college)

Flannery O'Connor tells us that the character Julian "appeared pinned to the door frame, waiting like Saint Sebastian for the arrows to begin piercing him." R.E.M.'s "Losing My Religion" music video depicts images of Saint Sebastian.

Okay, I forgot. My bad. That's me in the corner. Losing face.

steve

27 October 2007 – NYC
Steve,

I would *love* to leave you with this mistaken picture of me spending the last 40 years poring over *The Lives of the Saints*, but I have to come clean. My knowledge of Saint Sebastian comes primarily from art museums, where I've seen probably at least three dozen different depictions of the holey Sebastian.

For almost a thousand years (600-1600), it seems it was pretty much mandatory for any painter worth his salt to do 1) a Madonna and child, 2) an Annunciation and 3) a Saint Sebastian. As a result, when you go through any art museum, you'll see many versions of these scenes, usually called by those exact names. Today, of course those same paintings would be called, respectively: "Pre-Daycare," "The Rabbit Died," and "Custer at the Little Big Horn."

terry

27 October 2007 – Gilbert, AZ.
dear terry,

Wow, it's cool outside, in the morning at least, here in Arizona, and it's only October. I woke up early this morning with my mind still picturing the fire you will start in Mexico. So I had to get to the keyboard to write this down quickly. It might not make sense. (Has that ever stopped me?)

Do you follow ballet? I think not. I don't much either. To see you dance, I don't think you do. Last I saw you dance was in Halifax at your son's wedding reception. You follow Mick Jagger, is what we would conclude, watching you dance. But the great ballet master George Balanchine said something I want you to hear: "I've got more energy now than when I was younger because I know exactly what I want to do."

When you marveled at Jane Austen's having written those novels by the age of 25 I think the Balanchine factor (purpose) was already at play in her life. It took me about 58 years to know … really for sure … what I wanted to do. It took Jane fewer, but that's because she was clarified by a sense of focused purpose. In my opinion.

Tom Wolfe studied the life of the novelist Balzac because he wanted to know how Balzac was so productive. How he wrote so much! Wolfe said of Balzac, "I am convinced that the reason this genius was so productive – he published at least sixty books between the ages thirty and fifty-one – was that he enjoyed no time- or labor-saving devices whatsoever, not even a typewriter. He dropped nothing and went nowhere at a moment's notice."

We are victims of our own self-created, labor-saving abundance in America. We can entertain (in my case "distract from my mission") ourselves with countless delights. TV. Movies. Plays. Galleries (to see the various classic Saint Sebastian paintings). Etc. Ben Folds has a great song about this called "All U Can Eat." In the song he sings about overweight American people in SUVs driving around buying absolutely unnecessary things. His song's conclusion is:

God made us number one because he loves us the best
Well maybe He should go bless someone else for a while, give us a rest

Steve

29 October 2008 – NYC, NY
Steve,

Wolfe can have his Balzac for inspiration; I'll take Anthony Trollope. If you read his autobiography you cannot help but be overwhelmed by his work ethic.

Like many of us, he used to set himself a schedule of writing a number of hours per day, but he didn't stop there. He also demanded from himself 150 words every 15 minutes. So in a two-hours session, he'd wind up with a minimum of 1200 words!

I don't know about you, but when I'm really going good, I turn out about 300 words an hour and feel very pleased with myself. Trollope did that every *half* hour.

My favorite story about him is one time when he was on a cruise, but still doing his writing hours, he reached "The End" of one of his three-volume, 750-page novels after an hour and forty-five minutes of a two hours session.

With the remaining 15 minutes, he wrote the first 150 words of his next novel!

Me? I would have been tempted to knock off for the day, maybe pour myself a glass of champagne.

Terry.

1 November 2007 – Gilbert, AZ. 85234
ter.

We've come a long way from the time when Mary Ann Evans had to disguise herself as George Eliot to get her novels published. Women today earn millions from their creative writing! Just last night (Halloween) my grandson, who is seven years old, showed up at my doorstep dressed as Harry Potter. (The figment of a very creative woman's imagination.)

In this book it is becoming apparent that the problem of pride is personified by Mr. Darcy, who although falsely accused of being a bad guy is too proud to stoop to defend himself. Pride constricts him and ties him in knots so he can look like the strong and silent type. I wish he were more open in his communications. Not a totally feminized metrosexual, but at least enough to explain himself and stand up for himself more openly.

The wildly pompous, insecure and obsequious Mr. Collins is also a personification of pride. But he is pride run riot. Pride blown up into strange exaggerations of the male ego to the point of comic absurdity.

The character I like the most to this point is Mr. Bennet, the father. He is amused and amusing. Of course it may seem that Mr. Bennet is frivolous or irresponsible by never taking any of his wife's or children's romantic misadventures seriously. Some may even think he avoids his fatherly responsibilities by always retiring to his study to read while the others are arguing all of life's dramas. But I think he is the voice of bemused wisdom. Perhaps he is Jane Austen herself at a higher level than even the narrator.

Maybe because Jane Austen never married and became one of the most highly valued authors of all time (by valuing her own independence, talent and passion) she was in a wonderful position to expose this frantic man-chasing for the comedy of errors that it was. This book so far is the story of wealth and the story of social standing always getting in the way of two people really meeting and loving each other.

Not that times have changed so much. People will still "fall in love" with a story rather than a person. Look at Jackie Kennedy and Aristotle Onassis or look at Princess Diana and Dodi Fayed. Stories hooking up with stories. No real people meeting each other.

I think the modern phenomenon of "trophy wives" occurs because of this. Presidential candidate Fred Thompson was interviewed on TV the other night with his wife who looked like his granddaughter. The man likes the story of a younger, more beautiful woman confirming his enduring attraction. The trophy wife herself is in love with the story of total financial security with her father-figure of a husband on her arm. Stories falling for stories.

Jane Austen uncovered this farce long ago and wrote so entertainingly about it that we love what we are reading. Mr. Bennet sees it too, and adds some humor to the mix, then retires to his study for a little brandy and a good book. My man.

s.

2 November 2007 – NYC
s.

Truman Capote once said, "All literature is gossip."

In the twenty years after *In Cold Blood* until his death Capote swore he was hard at work on his greatest work. It was to be called *Answered Prayers* and he claimed it would be the great novel of gossip.

In fact, the evidence points to his never having written any more of the book than the few pieces that appeared as excerpts in *Esquire*. Those chapters were loaded with gossip but it appeared that rather than the juicy bits being the product of Capote's imagination, they were instead the product of his stenography.

The Upper East Side babes who had delighted in telling him these scandalous stories over lunches at La Cote Basque were not as delighted when they read them in *Esquire*. They cut him off. And supposedly not a single person above 59th Street and east of the Park ever spoke to him again.

(Did the use of "babes" a couple of sentences back sound prejudicial and flippant? In my defense I can only point to the fact that the ringleader of those society harpies who cut off Capote's putative balls was actually *named* Babe – Babe Paley, wife of William Paley who was, at the time, CEO of CBS.)

Perhaps it was because his sources dried up that Capote was not able to complete the great gossip novel, but no great loss. To my mind the great gossip novel had already been published 150 years before Truman started his. And we're reading it with delight right now.

So very much of *Pride and Prejudice* is concerned with gossip. It's all, as you suggest, concerned with "stories" about the characters. In fact you could make the argument that the whole book is about what people in the neighborhood talk about and what they *might* talk about. Take our most recent twelve chapters (21-32), for instance, what has actually happened?

The Bingleys depart for London. Mr. Collins proposes to Charlotte and is accepted. The Gardiners visit the Bennets and then return to their unfashionable London address with Jane. Elizabeth travels to Hunsford to visit Charlotte. It all seems more like a description of strategic movements on a chessboard than the action of a novel. The other 90% of those chapters concerns itself with gossip and analysis of each of these modest actions.

Look at chapter 24. In the first sentence a letter arrives from Miss Bingley. The entire rest of the chapter is all talk about the contents of the letter – what was written, what wasn't and what both of those whats might mean.

Chapter 25 is much the same. The Gardiner's arrive at the Bennets' home in the second paragraph and the rest is *talk* – about what has happened, what might happen and what might happen after that.

Basically it's as much gossip as Capote's society ladies. But I do draw a big distinction between Capote's and Austen's gossip. When Capote's characters gossip, the reader is meant to be following the stories of those being gossiped about. The gossipers are merely a delivery system. Whereas in Austen, the gossip scenes are designed to reveal as much about the feelings and character of the gossipers as they are about the subjects of the gossip.

You know there have always been Jane Austen detractors who argue that she never really deals with the important events of the world. That she essentially wrote mere village marriage tales about silly 20-year-old girls in full pursuit of husbands.

Characterizing *P&P* as a book of small town gossip would seem to support this view. And it is true that there is not a single mention in the book of Parliament, the King or the Napoleonic Wars, which were hot news at the time.

I think Jane Austen's defense is as simple as that's not the novel she wanted to write.

In the context of the book, who cares who the Prime Minister was or who was King? And in this novel, the only reason we even care about Napoleon is that because of the fear of a French invasion, the regiment is stationed at Meryton. If it weren't for Napoleon's ambition, there would be no Wickham.   t.

3 November 2007 – Arizona
wow Terry-

Sobering message from you. Thanks for the Capote quote on gossip … and the inside scoop on his final pathetic "work." If that's all Capote's book was about then we can truly thank God for un*Answered Prayers*. I'm glad he didn't finish it.

Capote finished his life drunk. People like him get writing and drinking confused. They think they are writers but they are drinkers. They think they are using their lives for "creating" but they are using their lives for destroying. It's like getting up and down mixed up. You think you're moving up when you're really falling down. It's like getting life and death mixed up.

Finally the writer like Capote or Kerouac or Dylan Thomas (the list is endless, and your father wrote eloquently about Malcom Lowry on this subject) is thinking he is LIVING his novel! All the gossip and adventures and profound and meaningful parties. A moveable feast of a novel being LIVED instead of written. So life, in this case, is confused with death. Because the life of the party is really the death of the writer.

I experienced this all too painfully in my years as an alcoholic, living wildly and clutching to crumpled wine-stained notebooks filled with poetic writings I either made drunk or hung over. It was just disgustingly awful writing, but I thought I was living something very colorful. I was not. I was the skeleton at the feast of death. And nothing was moveable in my spirit at all.

Truman Capote began as a beautiful writer and ended up as a repulsive little bon vivant. Alcohol is not complicated. Nor are the people who live off of it.

s.

3 November 2007 – NYC
Steve,

You bring up Lowry; I am currently reading his *Under the Volcano*. This novel has been named one of the ten best novels in English in the 20th century. It is also, of course, hailed as the ultimate alcoholic novel.

I cannot understand its reputation.

You write of how awful your under-the-influence poetry was, I wish someone had applied the same critical eye to Lowry's work. It is simply not interesting reading the meditations of a drunk. They are too warped – too incoherent.

There isn't much mention of drinking at all in Jane Austen. And yet I cannot believe there was any less of it in her time than ours. I read in my *Annotated P&P* that port was the drink of choice in Jane's day. That should certainly have been enough to keep those Regency gents sober. Port's always been way too sweet to have much of.   terry.

4 November 2007 – Arizona
Dear Ter,

I had to laugh this morning when I woke up and read an email from an army Captain stationed at Fort Bragg. Let me tell you why …

A year or so ago at your home in Mexico, you and I were kicking around all kinds of ideas for what our third "Two Guys" book would be and you jokingly threw out "*Two Guys Read the Q'uran?*" But then you nixed the idea, saying we'd probably have to go underground like Salman Rushdie or those people who drew those cartoons about Mohammed because radical Islam has yet to develop a refined sense of humor.

Now I wake up and find that a U.S. Army Captain writes this to me today: "I went to West Point and have deployed to both Iraq and Afghanistan since 2004 and will be headed over again in 2008. Near the end of my last rotation to Afghanistan, I ordered your book *100 Ways to Motivate Yourself* and have become a huge fan of your work. Since then, I have purchased over 50 copies of that book and *Reinventing Yourself* to send to my family and friends – most specifically, those who have been sent overseas."

I mention this to you as a warning because if these books ever did fall into enemy hands, we might still risk decapitation. Of course, when you think about it, this may result in the public making these books huge posthumous bestsellers. Who will you leave your royalties to? Let's not leave them to our families because our families don't read our books. Isn't that the sad truth? They get enough of us in real life. Boy will they feel bad when they see the *fatwah* issued against our lives.

s.

5 nov 07 – New York, NY
steve,

Actually, my family is pretty good about reading my books. Of my brothers, Tony's not much of a reader, but Chato's read almost all of my stuff – and commented favorably. He even liked my mystery novel (as you know, unpublished). This puts him high on my list of most astute literary critics.

And both Andrew and Lincoln [*The author's sons. TNH*] have at least dipped into chunks of our books. I know this because I occasionally spring little ambush tests on them.

Their wives, however ... well, as you say, for the most part, they can't be bothered. I'm certain this will all turn around now that we've taken up Jane Austen as our subject. Soon, I'm sure, my brothers' and sons' wives will be organizing a "Two Guys" fan club.

Our *own* wives, however, have been exemplary fans and I know they read our books for the sheer enjoyment. I can't believe they're at all influenced by potential royalties or the psychological bribe of dedications.

You mentioned on the phone the other day that since we started reading Jane it really seems that this has become the "Year of the Woman." Nonsense. This is merely the same phenomenon we noticed when we wrote *Two Guys Read Moby-Dick*: Suddenly we were overwhelmed by a shower of *Moby-Dick* sightings. References to Melville or the novel popped up everywhere. Of course, they had always been there, it was merely our heightened awareness while working on the book that made us see them.

Likewise women with this book. My research indicates that women have been present in virtually every era of recorded time. Biological science backs me up on this.

t.

9 november 2007 – arizona
dear terry,

I agree with what you said about the Napoleonic wars. Jane Austen didn't need to write about the war to help us understand war. She is brilliant at comedically dramatizing how the stupidity of pride and the nastiness of prejudice can stop people from connecting with each other. The love affair of Elizabeth and Mr.

Darcy is particularly captivating because of how many inner obstacles they conquer to find their love for each other.

By illuminating what happens inside the human mind when it believes narrow things, Jane Austen is as good as *War and Peace*. War actually happens because of pride and prejudice. If you don't understand it at the level of the individual, then you'll never solve it at the level of nations or warring religions.

Jane Austen is brilliant writing about that battle within. Darcy is conquering his earlier prejudice about Elizabeth's lower social standing and revealing himself to be a noble person. And the characters in this novel that are looking outside themselves to fulfill their fantasies (of, say, financial security through marriage) are made to be ridiculous.

As to the drinking port wine in Jane Austen's day ... On the streets of American inner-cities, back in the day, white port flowed freely. To alcoholics like me white port was cheap and therefore a great wine to always have around. (Which I almost always did.) In the neighborhoods people cut the sweetness of the port wine with lemon juice, which is how the great old doo-wop song "White Port and Lemon Juice" came into being. The Four Deuces recorded a 78 rpm vinyl recording of "WPLJ" ("Ooooo what it do to you!") in the '50s and it was later covered by Frank Zappa. I was at a friend's house in Fresno not long ago and he pulled that Four Deuces 78 from his classic collection and played it! Better than Zappa!

You and I have been lucky, Terry, in that our first two books together have gotten some good reviews, both in newspapers and on Amazon. There have been a couple of misguided exceptions where people were expecting something more self-improving from me, but in general the reviews have been gratifying enough to make this book here a reality.

I don't actually mind getting bad reviews now and then, especially when they are accurate and well-thought out like this one that appeared on Amazon for my book *17 Lies* (audiobook version). Reviews like this allow me to learn and grow:

A Review of Steve Chandler's
17 Lies That Are Holding You Back And the Truth That Will Set You Free
(Audio CD)

What A Bunch Of Bull!

This was a horrible book. I bought this audio book because of all the positive feedback that I read. I listened to it and could not believe what an idiot the author is. He goes on and on about things he thinks he knows something about and therefore considers himself an expert. He is so full of himself and boring. His monotone voice is enough to make you want to shoot yourself.

The only truth that will set you free is to know that this audio book isn't worth a darn and that the author is making a fortune spreading his bull around.

M. Wilson

It was great seeing you in New York last week and actually seeing the two different versions of *Pride and Prejudice* you are reading from (one annotated, one not.) You inspired me to get a new second version not annotated and my reading is much swifter and happier now. Amazing how notations can cause you to lose the whole rhythm of Jane Austen's wit.

Well, I have to run and spend some of that now-shameful fortune I've made on *17 Lies* getting ready for Thanksgiving. I hope you and Miranda have a happy one. We have a lot to be thankful for this year. s.

15 Nov 07 – New York
steve,

These latest chapters are largely concerned with Elizabeth's trip to Hunsford – the visit with the newlyweds Charlotte and Mr. Collins. Of course, it turns out that that pompous prig Darcy is also in the vicinity visiting his aunt. And this confluence results in the wonderful scene of Darcy's proposal to Elizabeth in chapter 34.

I can think of no other scene in all of literature (or at least the literature I've read) I remember more clearly than this one. The haughty Darcy admitting his utter helplessness in the face of a woman of no consequence. And then Elizabeth's spirited and beautifully phrased rejection.

The scene is not only memorable, it is also the turning point in the novel. It is the high water mark of misunderstanding between Darcy and Elizabeth, for starting in the very next chapter with Darcy's umbrage letter, the blindfolds of pride and prejudice begin to lift.

From my previous readings, I knew *exactly* what was going to happen when I started the chapter and still I thrilled to it. But I'd be interested in your reaction. Did you know from having seen the movie versions of the book what Darcy was going to do?

You know who I find interesting? Charlotte Lucas/Collins. I think she's a very strong and admirable character. And I'm not at all sure that Jane Austen likes her as well as I do. I think Jane's feelings would be more in line with Elizabeth's, who was horrified that Charlotte would agree to, what she assumes could only be, a loveless marriage to Mr. Collins. Elizabeth sees it as a total sellout.

Don't you think there's a bit of a double standard on Elizabeth's part here?

After all, she is more than understanding when Wickham turned his attentions away from her and instead focuses on Mary King who has just come into an inheritance. Or witness her attitude toward Colonel Fitzwilliam, who despite being attracted to Elizabeth, makes it clear that he cannot possibly marry her because she has no money. In both these instances, she not only doesn't blame them for these actions, she comes close to admiration for their pragmatism.

And yet … when Charlotte makes a similarly pragmatic move in accepting Mr. Collins, Elizabeth excoriates her. Charlotte's a woman who knows what she wants. And when the opportunity presents itself, she goes out and gets it. She wants to run a home of her own and to be comfortable financially.

She is also fully aware that the price she'll pay to get these things is living with an ass-kissing buffoon of a husband. She knows what she wants. She knows the price. And she's prepared to make the deal.

Compare her acceptance of Mr. Collins just as he unfortunately is with Mary Bennet's attitude back in chapter 22 when she thinks *she* might be a candidate for a Mr. Collins proposal. Mary believes that he might make a "very agreeable companion" after she improves him a bit and encourages him to read more.

This is I think a common flaw in women: They believe in the perfectibility of man.

Specifically the man they intend to marry.

They never marry the man before them; they marry the man they think they can turn him into.

Men don't think this way. And are happier for it. Whereas women wind up being very unhappy when, five years down the line, they find they are living with the same flawed guy who was supposed to have changed by now.

Men are often accused of putting their wives on a pedestal. Women build a pedestal and then spend their time trying to create something worthy of going on it.

The whole relationship between Elizabeth and Charlotte is interesting. We are told they are best friends and yet there is a big difference in their ages: Elizabeth is 20 and Charlotte 27. Obviously they are both intelligent and that is a bond, but still how many 20-year-olds would you have considered "best friend candidates" when you were 27?

The credit for the care and feeding of the friendship belongs with Charlotte I suspect. Not only was she perspicacious in spotting Elizabeth's qualities when she was just a girl, but she also refuses to give up on her just because their outlooks on life are so demonstrably different.

When Charlotte agrees to marry Collins, Elizabeth sees her as "disgraced" and can't believe they will ever be close again. It is Charlotte who makes a point of being the first to break the news to Elizabeth; she also forces Elizabeth to *promise* to visit her in

Hunford. And, of course, it is this, of course, that gives us that wonderful chapter 34.

t.

19 November 2007 – Gilbert, Arizona
Dear Terry,

Yes, I had seen the movie version, or at least the BBC Colin Firth-as-Mr. Darcy version of this book – which was absolutely great – but, no, I still wasn't really ready for Darcy's proposal.

They had been so distant from each other previously, pridefully jousting with words. (Haven't we all done that negative kind of flirtation in life? I've never seen it captured as well as this.) We knew Darcy was mesmerized by Elizabeth, and we knew Elizabeth was reluctantly fascinated with him but repelled by the stories she'd heard about him and his original snobbish refusal to ask her to dance in the early scene.

And previous to this scene the whole book is more amusing than anything else. So you're not ready for this scene. Darcy shows up to talk to her and they are alone and he sits for awhile and then gets up and begins pacing around the room and then just blurts out, "In vain I have struggled. It will not do. My feelings will not be repressed. You must allow me to tell you how ardently I admire and love you."

And then, later, her rejection – so well-stated and so full of self-righteous certainty that Darcy has been an unfair and unkind man to have broken up his friend's relationship with her beloved older sister, and having financially betrayed the poor, charming military officer Mr. Wickham. How could she marry a man who was so rude and without conscience?

He leaves totally devastated. He is so shocked by her accusations that he can't even gather himself to answer. And Elizabeth is so smart and stingingly, bitingly eloquent in her soliloquy of rejection that Darcy is rather floored. It reminded me of what used to happen when a poorly educated liberal would show up on William F. Buckley's *Firing Line* television show.

But Darcy's speechlessness is not poor education, for we've heard him formulate his arguments earlier in articulate ways. He's just stunned. So he leaves. He retreats for a day and composes himself and writes the letter! Now right here in the book is where I am most blown away by Jane Austen. Although the proposal scene is surely one of literature's finest. The next two chapters are the ones that most took my breath away. I mean that literally. First, his letter. (And it had to be a letter. If he had said all those well-reasoned arguments that defended his actions it would have been absurd and unrealistic. Jane Austen was brilliant to have Darcy put it in a letter.)

My jaw dropped in the next chapter when Elizabeth reads and re-reads the letter, re-reading each sentence and looking back on her experience to see where she had been wrong every step of the way about Mr. Darcy. Her tears and self-hatred and remorse are so real.

But what's most heartbreaking is that she can see that her own vanity led to all of this. It was more than just a misunderstanding. It was shallow girlish vanity for the character that had supposed herself the deepest and wisest of everyone she knew. Her vanity led to her stupid, erroneous conclusions. Her wanting to be danced with. Her being flattered and charmed by the lying Mr. Wickham's attention to her. All the things she despised most in others were her own worst flaws.

I think Jane Austen is ahead of her time in her understanding of psychology. (Another example of art being way out ahead of science.) Her ability to have us live, through Elizabeth, all the stages of realization of how the false ego (the one so easily charmed and misled by others because of its need for identity and gratification) misleads the soul. I can't remember any novel ever having such a bold, romantic and beautiful turning point as this one, in which the ego is stripped bare and two souls remain, facing each other. In those moments only love can be there.

Last evening I attended a little family birthday gathering and my daughter Mar had given me some Jane Austen-related gifts, knowing we were working on this book right now. (A CD of readings from her novels by Helena Bonham Carter, and a very fascinating book called *What Jane Austen Ate and Charles Dickens Knew: From Fox Hunting to Whist – the Facts of Daily Life in 19th Century England.*) And we talked about what it was like reading a Jane Austen novel. (Mar is a big fan.) We agreed that it took a little while to get into the language, and the cadence of the writing. It is very cerebral. Not densely cerebral, but elegantly cerebral. But once you acclimate yourself to the flow of the language, it is addictive. Jane Austen's writing becomes more captivating with each new chapter because of how many layers of psychological posturing she strips away.

And to those macho guys who are too tough to read anything softer than a violent crime thriller I say you are missing a lot if you don't read Jane Austen.

One thing a novel can do is go deep into the psyche of the character. Deeper still to the heart and soul of human motivation. Movies can suggest things in a visually glorious way, but they can't take you all the way in.

Sometimes a movie will try. They will do a "voice over" from the novel as we watch a peaceful visual scene. The actor will read from a page that the director thought could only be captured by the writing. But it fails. It takes you out of the medium you are in. It breaks the spell of the movie you have been watching. It doesn't really work. A good book in a quiet room is still the most profound experience known of one person's art being downloaded into another human being's mind. Nothing compares. As Chapters 34, 35 and 36 prove.

Oh, a final note here, about how popular Jane Austen now is. A friend of ours gave Kathy and me a gift the other day. The gift was a Jane Austen action figure! I'm not kidding. It's a great plastic action figure (just like the ones you see in toy stores for Superman and Spiderman). There's a quill you can put into her hand and a sheaf of parchment for her to write on.

Have a wonderful Thanksgiving in Los Angeles, which is where I believe you said you'd be, Steve

Nov20 – Los Angeles, CA
Steve,

Yes, we're out here in Hollywood, which is the proper place from which to weigh in on your comments on the use of "voice over" in film.

I told you earlier that there have been nine different film versions of *Pride and Prejudice*. I'll bet you every one of them uses a voice-over. This is a total guess on my part; in fact, I don't know for certain that even *one* of them uses a voice-over. But it is a shrewd guess based on my well-known deep understanding of human nature.

If you were a director or a screenwriter, could you resist including the opening line of the novel in your film? And how could you possibly do it except as a voice-over? It's too carefully constructed to ever pass as credible dialogue.

In the serious film world there is a general prejudice against voice-over. It's seen as an easy way to get out of story problems, a cheap device that isn't really "filmic." I have several times been told this by film directors I worked with in Canada. In that country no director wants to make a "movie," they all want to make a "film." Commercial success is pretty much seen as failure there. This is, of course, one of the main reasons Canada boasts so few commercially successful films.

This is not to say that they don't make terrific films – they do. I cite *Away From Her*, the Sarah Polley film, as a prime example – an absolutely wonderful film that no one's ever heard of. But it *is* to say that these are "serious" filmmakers and they would put up a strong fight before ever giving in to allow a voice-over. And yet I feel certain they would surrender in the face of Jane's opener.

(By the way, I find it interesting that a lot of these anti-voice-over film people rave about *Apocalypse Now*, which has Martin Sheen doing mucho voice-over.)

t.

21 November 2007 – Gilbert, Arizona

Terry,

Some time back, you asked what I thought of Charlotte Lucas – Elizabeth's cousin who marries the ridiculous Mr. Collins for money. Well, first of all I noticed that one of the 40 sequels that have been written to *Pride and Prejudice* by other authors (that's a true fact! 40! I read it on the back of the box that contained my Jane Austen action figure!) is called *Consequence: Whatever Became of Charlotte Lucas?* The book got poor reviews on Amazon.

I tend to like Charlotte, too. Very practical woman. And in her day it wasn't easy to have much of a life if you were an unmarried woman. It's not like she could start an at-home internet business. It would take the bravery of a Jane Austen to stay single on principle and reject every suitor who wasn't Colin Firth.

As to your wry observation that women put men on a pedestal and then get disappointed when the men turn out to be imperfect, singing Hank Williams' "Take Me As I Am Or Not At All," and never change as the women hoped. First of all I think men do this too! I have male friends who talk to me about how their wives aren't living up to their (the men's) expectations. How they've "let themselves go" while shifting all their attention from the man to the kids. So there's plenty of disappointment to go around when you play the expectation game.

I say expect nothing! Let everything be a pleasant surprise. Stop judging the other person. Let them be whoever they please. That's what I say.

Alan Watts, when he was a minister, used to perform marriage ceremonies. He had one pre-nuptial question he asked the couple prior to performing the ceremony: "Are either one of you entering into this marriage hoping the other person will change or improve themselves in any way? If so, I will not perform this ceremony, because your marriage will not work."

Steve

22 Nov 2007 (Thanksgiving) – Los Angeles, California
steve

You mention attending "a little birthday gathering" several days ago. I blithely read through that, following the Jane Austen thread you were writing about and it never occurred to me until now that was *your* birthday. So I missed it again, damn! Well, a belated happy birthday, Steve.

Missing your birthday, means that I also missed a friend of mine's whose birthday is the day after yours. I always tell her I'll never forget her birthday because it's so linked with yours. This is true, of course, unless I forget yours. As I seem to have done.

And naturally you and everyone else of our generation remember what happened 44 years ago today. That's right, it was the day that *both* Aldous Huxley and C.S. Lewis died. Both got shamefully scant attention in the newspapers the following day.

Later, Sheryl Crow wrote a song ("Run, Baby, Run") which opens with the lines: "She was born in November 1963 / The day Aldous Huxley died." It's interesting that there is no mention of the death of JFK in the song. It merely assumes that everyone knows that Huxley died the day Kennedy was assassinated.

And while I'm on the subject of songs, let me correct you on the song "Take Me as I Am or Not at All."

First off, the song is called "Take Me as I Am or Let Me Be."

Second, Hank Williams neither wrote nor sang that song. It was written by a guy named Boudleaux Bryant in 1954. Hank died, famously, on New Year's Eve 1953.

I'm going to let you off the hook on that one in exchange for you letting me off the hook on missing your birthday.

And now that I've finished the little housekeeping digressions, what I set out intending to write you about was Elizabeth. You say you love her for being a ferocious romantic. Well, so do I. But you know what else I love about her? She ain't no goody two-shoes.

Even though she always strives to think and do right, she's still human enough to take gleeful delight in each setback Miss Bingley suffers in her attempts to make a match with Mr. Darcy.

Now the reader already knows that Miss Bingley is a bitch from seeing her backroom backstabbing when the Bennet sisters aren't around. But even if I didn't know this, I'd still love Elizabeth for her delicious enjoyment of the younger Miss Bingley's thwarted schemes. It's clear Miss Bingley doesn't like her and Lizzy is human enough to not like her right back.

t.

25 November 2007 – Gilbert, AZ.

Terry,

So here's a difference between us. You're a true film person and I'm more of a movie guy. You watch a lot of art films, you've written and directed I-don't-know-how-many commercials, documentaries, etc. You visit art galleries, go to many plays every year, and take in elevated culture constantly.

Me? I'm waiting for the next Bourne movie. That will give you a good perspective.

So when you say that *Away From Her* is a fantastic film I have to just take your word for it because I bailed on it after about 15 minutes! Watching someone lose her marbles from Alzheimer's was so depressing I couldn't stand it. Even more marbles dropping out of her in greater frequency as the film rolled on.

I know I should be more grown up about it. Of course I know that people die. You have to die somehow. And people are always going to lose a step or two. The wheels do come off the bus. It's old age; I know that. But here I am with my popcorn looking forward to a Julie Christie movie remembering how great she was in *McCabe and Mrs. Miller* and in *Dr. Zhivago* and all of a sudden she's losing her mind.

I'm glad your parents and mine did not die that way. Your dad in fact was writing witty newspaper columns right up till the end of his life. He even wrote one just after he died! (Or maybe wrote it a week or so before he died and pretended it was just after. It was so good though … and now I want to share it here, but we don't have the space so I'll put it on my website and readers can read it if they want. They can just go to the contact page and ask me for it. Art Hill from beyond the grave.)

So I now know I bailed on a very fine film! Just because I was getting depressed. And now from reading the news today I realize that I might have stayed with that film had I not been eating popcorn. Had I been eating salmon and walnuts I might have been far less gloomy. For it seems that foods that contain high quantities of omega-3 fatty acids and/or a nutrient called uridine, such as salmon, herring, walnuts, sugar beets, and beet molasses, have natural depression-fighting qualities, according to a research report published in *Biological Psychiatry*. The report said that scientists have long known that nations consuming large quantities of fish had low levels of both heart problems and clinical depression.

(What were you eating when you watched Michigan lose to Ohio State last week?)

And, wow, this is even more interesting: a new study comes from William Carlezon Jr., Ph.D., and colleagues from McLean Hospital's Psychiatry Department. It shows that injecting listless, unmotivated rats with uridine and omega-3 (found in salmon and walnuts) caused the rats to RISE UP and complete tasks and finish running through mazes they had previously given up on. The rats stopped being quitters. That's the food for me!

One thing I admire about the films, plays and galleries you see regularly is that your retirement is so colorful and active. You travel all over. You even live in two or three different places each year. You keep journals and notebooks that chronicle your life, track a writing discipline that has you write at least one hour each day and do the power walk religiously (and track and record that, too.) Contrast that to the retirement mode we are most familiar with. The one that involves little more than the channel changer and the doctor visits. In some ways, you've actually picked UP the pace of your life with retirement.

How does all of this relate to Jane Austen? Jane never lived long enough to get Alzheimer's. The medical care in her age was so abominable that new research shows that people back then had a better chance of recovery if a doctor *failed* to show up to care for them. Medicine did more harm than good. (As it often does today, just not at that alarming rate.) But while other women spent their spare time playing whist and gossiping, Jane retired to her room (like you) and wrote and wrote.

s.

5 December 2007 – Back in New York
steve,

I was just re-reading your last, and must say I find your characterization of me hilarious. Do I put up such a good front that you cannot see the rickety beams and baling wire that prop up the façade?

In the first place I am only occasionally as disciplined as you suggest. You can usually find me listed in the top three or four in both the AP and computer polls of the nation's leading procrastinators. And secondly, I'm waiting for the next Bourne film too. But as for *Away From Her*, I stand by my opinion – though I'm with you in generally staying away from depressing films.

Iris, for instance was a depressing film. Miranda wanted to see it so we went, and while I will say I *admired* it, I hated watching it. They can say "life-affirming" all they want, but it dragged me down. I thought *Away From Her*, on the other hand, escaped mass audience suicides with its matter-of-fact acceptance of reality and some very funny scenes.

(And I'll make you this bet: Julie Christie will be nominated for an Academy Award. The recent revelation of Sandra Day O'Connor's husband finding a new babe in his Alzheimer's haze will revive notice of this film which, by traditional thinking, came out too early in the year for the usual award nomination hype.) [*Several months later Julie Christie <u>was</u> nominated for Best Actress in the Academy Awards. She did not, however, win. TNH*]

Anyway, we're back from LA and, yes, I'm behind schedule commenting on the chapters 43-49. (See second paragraph of this letter above re: procrastination.) These chapters of the book are dominated first by Elizabeth's visit to Pemberley and the sea change in Mr. Darcy, who is now meeting Elizabeth's standards more than halfway. But soon these pleasant actions are overwhelmed by the horror of Wickham's luring the stupid Lydia into the country of fallen women.

Lydia does seem to lead a charmed life though, and after an anxiety-fraught couple of weeks, the silly thing falls into a bed of roses. She becomes, at 15 or 16, the youngest of the Bennet girls to capture a husband – that being the admirable Wickham.

Yes, of course, Wickham is a totally unprincipled jerk, but in chapter 48 we are given ample evidence to convince us that he is only the second worst of the possible Bennet sister suitors we've seen. The worst – and running away with the title – would be the awful Mr. Collins, whose condescending letter to Mr. Bennet flies under a false flag of consolation. In fact, it all but congratulates himself on having avoided marrying into Mr. Bennet's tainted family when Elizabeth turned him down.

Though I've merely summarized the story here, I hope in the telling you get some sense of the intense enjoyment and participation I experienced in the reading. I am consciously pulling for Darcy and Elizabeth to find each other; I am hating Mr. Collins; and I never intend to speak to that cad Wickham again. It is really quite amazing to me that Austen can get me this involved in the story … again. It's not as if I don't know how it all ends; I mean I *have* read the book three times before. And yet here I am again absolutely wrapped up in the fates of the characters and thrilling to the sentences.

I noticed one interesting effect of reading and thinking about *Pride and Prejudice* when I was in Los Angeles. As you know, we were staying with Miranda's sister Eunice and her husband and I caught myself paying a lot of attention to the relationship between the sisters. This is entirely due to spending so much time noting the relationship between Elizabeth and Jane in the book.

I never had sisters or daughters so it was interesting to me. You had two sisters and are father to three daughters so you've obviously had a lot of opportunity to see sisters together, but I've had little. I didn't put them under a microscope or anything; it's just that I was much more aware of their attachment than I had been in the past.

Nor am I saying Miranda and Eunice's relationship is the same as Jane and Elizabeth's. For one thing, there would be 200 years' difference between the two sets of sisters. The role of women has so dramatically altered in that time that it has to have had an effect on sisterly relations. Another big difference is that there is only a two-year difference in age between Jane and Elizabeth, while Miranda is twelve years older than Eunice. But the bond of sisters is still so very evident.

Miranda, as the older sister, helped bring Eunice up and has loved her and doted on her since babyhood. For her part, Eunice has always admired and almost idolized Miranda in a way Miranda will sometimes modestly downplay in company but I know personally finds extremely gratifying. To watch them together talking, laughing, cooking is wonderful. The devotion they show each other puts me in mind of Mr. Darcy's admiring notice of Elizabeth's devotion to Jane when Jane was ill at Netherfield early in the novel.

Miranda and Eunice are separated by some 3000 miles, but they are in constant e-mail communication and talk on the phone at least once a week, often for more than an hour at a time. They are as much in each other's confidence as Jane and Elizabeth were. Another similarity in the two pairs is in the common ambivalent relationships with their mothers. (Ah, daughters and mothers! I don't think this book will be long enough to cover that territory.)

As someone who's seen more of these relationships than I, do you think sisterly relations may in some ways be easier than brothers? I'm not sure why I say that – less competitive perhaps?

Terry.

12 Dec. 2007 – Gilbert AZ.

Dear Terry,

Sisters! A great song from the movie *White Christmas*, wasn't it? We watch that movie every other year. We used to watch it every year but it was too much. We began saying the lines along with the movie and therefore found it to be more fun to skip a year and plug in *The Bishop's Wife* with David Niven and Cary Grant as the alternate.

Sisters! (Jane Austen writes about complex family dynamics so well, so bitingly funny.)

Autobiographical flashback alert: I remember just getting sober, my life a lonely wreck, going to 12-step meetings, this was about 28 years ago, and I remember longing … LONGING … for female companionship. Be careful what you long for. Because three years later I had a wife and three daughters! Instant major, comprehensive coverage in the category of female companionship.

So I remember my girls and what sisters they were and are to each other. How sweet it was and has been. And I agree with you, it's a lot like Jane and Elizabeth in our book … maybe easier to do than brothers who are taught a more competitive approach. Scrapping for attention and approval.

But not all sisters all the time are Elizabeth and Jane or Eunice and Miranda. Consider Elizabeth and Lydia! Elizabeth can't stand it that the passionate young Lydia ran off with tricky Wickham, and then came home and was so fulsome and mindlessly boastful about being the only one of five sisters actually married. To her sisters Lydia is odious. Not to mention logorrheic. So. Not all sisters have that sweet bond.

Sandra O'Connor's husband John did me a big favor once. He brought me into his office in Phoenix and gave me a talk about becoming a writer. This was about 16 years ago. (He had offices in Phoenix, their home, and Washington DC.) He then put me in touch with a literary agent in Washington DC that he knew and many good things (and now 16 books later I am even more grateful) came out of that meeting. So can I forgive him now for "forgetting" who he's married to and falling in love again? Indeed I can.

(In one of the most underrated, entertaining and touching movies ever made, *Bye Bye Love*, Linda Ronstadt does a hauntingly beautiful version of "Falling In Love Again" on the soundtrack. If this book becomes a movie, it should be played right at this point.)

You told me recently, as you recounted your daily walk, there was snow crunching under your feet. We miss the seasons you have there. But at the same time I enjoyed being out in a lawn chair today in the sun.

Steve.

16 December 2007 – Jane Austen's birthday! – NYC
Steve,

I hated to see *Pride and Prejudice* end but there was so much joy in reading those final chapters (50 to 61). It is not just because I am a sucker for a happy ending and we are so satisfied with the happy outcomes in the fortunes of the characters we are most concerned with.

(In fact, there were tears of happiness in my eyes during much of reading these chapters. Yes, this is embarrassing, but I'd be macho-lying if I left it out. It's funny that while generally I think of myself as rational and unsentimental, I cry at virtually every movie I see. And, as I've just acknowledged, in many novels too. I am an equal opportunity weeper; I cry at the sad parts *and* at happy ones.)

But I also loved reading these chapters because we come to my favorite line in the book. And there it is – in the last paragraph of chapter 59. After all the mental anguish, wounded reputation and difficulties brought on the Bennet family by the unscrupulous and uncaring Wickham, Mr. Bennet surveys the fallout of three daughters suddenly acquiring husbands within the space of weeks, and musingly says to Elizabeth: "I admire all my sons-in-law highly. Wickham, perhaps, is my favorite." ! ! !

I have found the line so very funny every time I've read the book and yet it's almost impossible to explain its humor adequately to anyone who has not read the preceding 395 pages. Imagine a standup comic with an act in which he went through an eleven-hour buildup prior to delivering the punch line. Could be an interesting act.

I also love Mr. Bennet's line in the previous chapter: "For what do we live but to make sport for our neighbors, and laugh at them in our turn." This is, of course, much of what the entire novel is about.

In Carol Shields's biography of Jane Austen she mentions Elizabeth Bennet's "ravishing intelligence." A happy and accurate phrase I think. When you think about it there is almost no description of Elizabeth's looks in the book: yes, she is described generally as good looking and much is made of her lively eyes. But do you have a clue what color her hair is? (In fact she is always played as a brunette in films while her sister Jane is often blonde, but if the book gives us any information on this, I missed it.)

And yet I think of her as fatally attractive – as "ravishing." And this impression is created almost entirely by her brilliant words, the manifestation of her intelligence.

In many of Jane Austen's surviving letters she makes no bones of her affection for Elizabeth as a character, but she also is bothered by how perfectly she speaks. She's right of course, in fact we have difficulty thinking of many of those speeches being extemporaneous – they are too brilliant. I am personally very able to overlook this flaw (if flaw it is), but it troubled Jane. And she worked hard to eliminate these too facile conversations.

Austen essentially wrote three novels before she was 25: *Sense and Sensibility, Pride and Prejudice* and *Northanger Abbey*. None were published until she was 36. She wrote almost nothing between the ages of 25 and 35. And then from 35 to her death at 42 she wrote her final three. It is on these last three that she works hard at being more realistic and the speeches are never again so polished as Elizabeth's. Anyway, we are about to read one of those last three – *Mansfield Park*. I'll be very interested to see what you think. For my part, I think it's hard to top *Pride and Prejudice*.

Happy 232nd Birthday, Jane.

t.

17 December 2007 – Gilbert, Arizona
Dear Terry,

I am amazed at how much I loved reading *Pride and Prejudice*. I also was sorry it had to end. In some ways it's a shame that so many good movies have been made of the Austen books. Because they give the impression that she is all about love and romance and colorful flirting and manners.

What the movies cannot get to – or do justice to – is the intelligence. And not just the flashing sarcastic wit of Elizabeth and her father. But deeper still into intellectual courage and character. Like you, I loved Elizabeth's final encounter with the nasty elitist

Lady Catherine who tries to get our Lizzie to promise not to marry Darcy. This is even before Elizabeth is sure Darcy still wants her. She is so powerful in standing up to Lady Catherine over and over that it is actually inspiring to read! I challenge any military or spy novel to have such a scene where the hero is so airtight and eloquent in arguing her principles. So unstoppable.

When Darcy and Elizabeth finally both realize that they are in love and Elizabeth asks why he fell for her and what it was that attracted him, she says, "Now be sincere; did you admire me for my impertinence?"

Darcy says, "For the liveliness of your mind I did."

And indeed! For that is what we readers also admired her for the most. The liveliness of her mind. So what characterizes Jane Austen for me is that she is a novelist of the mind. A writer who captures beautifully the interplay of intelligences when they are challenged by love and status and money.

For those who say Jane Austen should have been writing about the Napoleonic wars that called Wickham to join the militia, they simply don't understand the depth of her writing. My collected books about Jane Austen are piling up around my desk as I become more and more interested in her. (I have you to thank for this, Terry. Thank you. Prior to this book I thought I knew all there was to know about Jane Austen from watching the movies. How deliciously humiliating!) In one of the books I discovered yesterday that in a letter to her niece Anna Austen, an aspiring novelist, Jane gave some advice about finding subject matter for a novel. She wrote, "three or four families in a country village is the thing to work on."

Because if you do that brilliantly, it's the microcosm of the whole world's human tragicomic state. We look to art to understand bigger things. Art is always ahead of science and history and psychology.

Looking back on this wonderful book ... a book about standing fearlessly and eloquently for love and independence in the face of status, money and prejudicial feelings, I have to nominate as the most moving moment being when Elizabeth reads the letter Darcy wrote her that explained and defended his behavior and exposed Elizabeth's completely false impressions of him.

She is so ashamed of herself, and so thoroughly critical of herself in having misjudged him, that I was even a little shocked to read it. Rarely has an author ever had her heroine be so wrong and so aware of being so wrong. "How despicably have I acted!" she cried. "I, who have prided myself on my discernment! I, who have valued myself on my abilities! Who have often disdained the generous candor of my sister, and gratified my vanity, in useless or blamable distrust. How humiliating is this discovery! Yet, how just a humiliation! Had I been in love, I could not have been more wretchedly blind. But vanity, not love, has been my folly. Till this moment, I never knew myself."

But this is also a great love story. This is true love, as the characters we like the most overcome obstacles to come together and marry in the end. And how beautifully it all comes together, like the end of the Beatles' "Abbey Road" album. Not like Shakespeare who had to use all kinds of awkward coincidences and supernatural interventions to bring characters together at the end. This novel weaves and completes like a good mystery.

People, at first, thought the Beatles were just a rock band that did Chuck Berry covers and had gimmicky mop top hairdos. Then the harmonies began to emerge. Wow. Then the odd chord sequences, and the poetic lyrics, and soon it was the most musically thrilling thing around. Jane Austen reminds me of them, in that her "rock and roll" pretense at the start is a romance novel. But then the harmonies emerge as you read. And the psychologically thrilling interplay of betrayals, misperceptions and money lust. There's a big difference between "Roll Over Beethoven" and "Eleanor Rigby."

Hoping you have the merriest Christmas ever, my gift from you was this book,

Steve

21dec07 – nyc
Steve.

Didn't it seem that there was a lot of explanation and plot-knot-tying after the real climax you mentioned in your last letter when Darcy and Elizabeth finally get on the same page and find out they're in love with each other? I've read some critics describing this as a weakness of the novel, that there are all these artificial conversations in which the lovers go over the past meeting by meeting and explain to each other what each was thinking at the time.

The critics complain it's all awkwardly constructed and too obviously designed to back-explain to the reader why things unfolded the way they did. They suggest that such clumsy carpentry is the mark of an inexperienced writer. Remember, they say, this was really Jane's first novel.

I feel very sorry for those critics; for they have unwittingly revealed that they've never had a true love affair. Because that is *exactly* what happens in that first rush of realization that you're in love with each other. You want to know everything the other person was feeling and thinking all through the sly, coded dance that led up to that revelation of mutual love: What did you really think when you met me the first time with my nose all red from a cold? When you told your sister that you weren't really interested in older guys, was that just a decoy? Why didn't you try to kiss me that afternoon we were left alone on the beach for two hours? Etc.

The point is you want to know it all. It is, after all, the novel of your life. Which is why that section did not feel at all contrived to me.

t.

22 dec 2007 – gilbert arizona

Dear Terry,

Yes I agree with you. The way Austen winds the book down, ties the knots, completes all the little stories, and paints the afterglow of falling in love is so welcome and fun to read. Otherwise it's over too soon.

(Sex is easy to write about … falling in love is nearly impossible to write about.)

Nabokov said the writer of genius knows how to make a novel a "controlled explosion." Which is the best description ever! The best writing is both explosive and controlled. Like the big bang itself.

You bring up the subject of critics and Jane Austen's writing. I have been fascinated reading them in recent weeks. Most are filled with praise. But there are some who are furious that she was so popular. Such as one H.W. Garrod.

Oh yes, it's the very same Heathcote William Garrod you are thinking of. The British classical literary scholar. He was Fellow of Merton College, Oxford for over 60 years. He was Oxford Professor of Poetry from 1923 to 1928. He was a serious player. And he ridiculed men – men like you and me – who loved reading Jane Austen. Garrod thought that a man who was content to read novels by "a mere slip of a girl," must be a womanish man. Garrod said that male admirers of Miss Austen have feminized themselves by loving a "sharp-tongued woman who fails to honor the virility of men."

Sounds to me like Garrod was awfully insecure. I really enjoy how much you like Jane Austen, that you cry when reading her books, and that you can still be a man. You can still chug a beer in a bar and shout expletives at the refs when they call one against the Michigan Wolverines. (And you were tearing up while reading Jane Austen that very morning in that little cafe on Bleecker Street.) Best of both worlds.

A man not afraid of the feminine principle becomes even more of a man. That's my theory. Men who not only have the strong, manly, virile thing going on but who also know how to express highly creative artistic intelligence. Those men end up being Muhammad Ali, dancing and reciting poetry while becoming the greatest boxer who ever lived, beating his opponents to a pulp while "floating like a butterfly." And Bruce Lee is another such man who incorporated the feminine principle into his martial arts and became the most feared fighter alive. Not a man? Hulk Hogan would never want to get into a ring with Bruce Lee. No male-only brute would ever survive against Bruce Lee.

And neither would Sir Heathcote William Garrod want to get into the ring in a celebrity death match against Jane Austen. She would beat him to a pulp with her superior mind. (Not to mention her parasol.)

You say you rank high in procrastination? I don't believe it! I've seen your precise performance-measuring notebooks, and a couple months ago in Detroit I called your hotel room from mine early one morning and asked Miranda if I could talk to you and she said I could catch you outside the hotel somewhere doing your daily, religious, never-to-be-put-off power walk. So I went outside and when I found you, you walked up to me and then kept jogging in place while we talked as you were a few minutes short of your allotted time. That's no procrastinator in my book.

But the book I'm reading now (as I take a break between *Pride* and *Mansfield*) is about a writer's procrastination. It's a wonderful funny book by Geoff Dyer called *Out of Sheer Rage*, a book about all the ways he puts off actually writing his proposed book about D.H. Lawrence.

Einstein said the time comes in life when we have read enough. It's time to stop reading. It's time to lay the books down and write. Whatever "writing" is for a person. He could have said the time for absorbing other people's work is over, it's time to CREATE something of your own. You can only be an apprentice for so long.

We entertain, inform, read and absorb ourselves to the drowning level. We may still see ourselves as apprentices. Like the apprentice a cobbler has in Hans Christian Anderson watching the craftsman make shoes. We take in albums, books, films, articles until our cups runneth over.

That's why I admired it that you went to a lot of plays, and then you actually *wrote* a play (that won an award). The time comes to actually make a shoe. To be the shoemaker you long to be.

"If Jack Nicklaus can win the Masters at 46, I can win the Kentucky Derby at 54," the great jockey Willie Shoemaker once said. Shoemaker also said, quite memorably, "Anybody with a little guts and the desire to apply himself can make it, he can make anything he wants to make of himself."

A favorite quote of mine from *The Wizard of Earthsea* by Ursula le Guin is this, and I read it to myself often, especially when I'm procrastinating (like you say you do when you don't) and she says this: "As a man's real power grows and his knowledge widens, ever the way he can follow grows narrower: until at last he chooses nothing, but does only and wholly what he must do."

I get shivers when I read that. It's a good time of year for shivers, so enjoy your Christmas in Connecticut!

Love to the lovely Miranda, too,
Steve.

22dec07 – NYC
Steve,

Your mention of Willie Shoemaker in your last letter reminds me that at one point, citing various accomplishments by women, you suggested that this might be called the Year of the Woman. Wasn't this even a big year for females in horseracing, you asked.

I guess you could make the distaff argument in horseracing based entirely on the exploits of one filly – Rags to Riches.

Normally the sexes don't race against each other in thoroughbred racing. Fillies don't usually compete in the big-name races like the Triple Crown (the Derby, the Preakness and the

Belmont Stakes), which are usually contested by colts. I say usually because fillies are *eligible*, it's just that they usually don't enter. There's a general feeling that the fillies aren't strong enough at three to challenge the males.

But there are exceptions. In fact, twice in the last thirty years a filly has actually won the Kentucky Derby – Winning Colors (1988) and Genuine Risk (1980). Before that the only filly to win the Derby was Regret in 1915. So in 133 years, only three fillies have won the Derby.

The most grueling Triple Crown race is the Belmont Stakes. At a mile and a half it's the longest of the three races and it comes at the end of a long campaign. No filly had won the Belmont since Tanya in 1905, 102 years ago.

Rags to Riches dominated the 3-year-old fillies and had no challenges left there so her owner and trainer said, "Why not?" And they entered her in the Belmont where she ran against six colts including Curlin who had won the Preakness three weeks earlier.

The stretch run was one of the most exciting I've ever seen and in the end Rags to Riches prevailed over Curlin by a head. I was thrilled and I think Jane would have been too (in a decorous way, of course.) We were at a dinner party with friends and I asked if we could watch the race (basically they had no choice, but they were great about it) and in the end I think they enjoyed that stretch run as much as I. The race put away, we retired to a really quite wonderful paella and conversation, but I kept replaying that stretch run in my mind. What a wonderful filly, that Rags to Riches!

In her next race, Rags to Riches injured herself and, though she is expected to return to racing sometime in 2008, she was definitely out for the year.

Guess who went on to win the Breeders' Cup Classic (the biggest race of the year)? Curlin – who was later named Horse of the Year. Horse of the year!?! Shit! Rags to Riches beat him like a drum – staring him in the eye, stride for stride, down the longest stretch run in the country.

Yeah, maybe it is The Year of the Woman.

terry.

23 December 2007 – Gilbert Arizona
Terry,

It's coming on Christmas and as I drive around town doing my final shopping for the festivities ahead I am listening to the James Taylor Christmas album in my car cranked up good and loud while I myself sing even louder as other drivers turn to look at the happy madman. James Taylor sings the song "River" by Joni Mitchell. Never thought of it as a Christmas song before but he sings "It's coming on Christmas, they're cutting down trees. They're putting up reindeer. And singing songs of joy and peace. Oh I wish I had a river I could skate away on."

Steve

24dec07 – New York, New York
Steve,

A couple of things about the writers you mentioned.

First, Geoffrey Dyer, who you mention as the author of *Out of Sheer Rage*. I think Dyer's a very interesting writer – he does it all: fiction, memoir, reportage, biography, criticism, travel, everything. I only wonder that I haven't come across a volume of his limericks.

This is, of course, more of a rarity in the U.S. than in England where Dyer is from. In the UK writers tend to cross literary genres largely as a matter of economic necessity, a curious desire to continue eating. It's simply a fact that the English market is only about a sixth of the size of our market, and since writers are basically paid by the number of readers they have, they tend to get a sixth of what a U.S. writer would get for the same work.

(Yes, I know I have grossly oversimplified the economics of writing. And there are in fact so many anomalies in the system that I couldn't begin to defend this proposition in any kind specific way in court. That, however, does not take away from the fact that the basic premise is undeniably valid.)

Anyway, as unfair as this may be to English writers, it has, for the better part of the last century, forced English writers to take on more – and different kinds of – work. So we have Graham Greene writing not just serious novels like *Brighton Rock*, but also the lighter "entertainments" (as he called them) like *Travels With My Aunt*, as well as travel books, spy thrillers, biography and political writing.

Dyer is like this too. I first read an almost scholarly piece he'd written on some subject; and then in New York several years ago I came across a modern novel by a Geoffrey Dyer called *Paris Trance* about a group of disaffected young people living in Paris. I bought and read the novel, but because the character of the work was so different from the first piece I half suspected there might actually be the coincidence of *two* Geoffrey Dyers. In fact, as far as I know, there aren't.

The second thing that caught my eye in your e-mail was your quoting Ursula Le Guin. She's a writer I've not read but I know of her, first because Miranda's read her, and second because, unlikely as this may seem, her work is one of the linchpins in the plot of the film *The Jane Austen Book Club*. You and Kathy should see that film.

Terry.

26 December 2007 – Gilbert, Arizona
Happy Holidays Terry,

Your comments on Elizabeth's ravishing intelligence and fatal attractiveness were right on the money with me. It has always fascinated me how a woman's mind can alter her physical appearance. (Both for better and for worse, depending on the nature of the mind.) For example, Barbra Streisand. I saw her in *Funny Girl* on Broadway when she was a new star. And if you just saw her, or a photo of her, without knowing her brilliant comic mind, without hearing her voice and her daring, intelligent interpretations of old songs like "Happy Days Are Here Again" you would not call her attractive. Yet her wit and her mind totally changed her appearance and soon she was sexy and stunning, even to look at!

I remember in college meeting certain young women who did not look, at first glance, all that alluring, but once they started talking and flirting and bantering if they were clever and creative and smart all of a sudden the whole appearance took on a new look. And that's exactly what happened to Darcy. When he first saw Elizabeth at the dance, he made a snide remark that she was rather plain, but after he started to get to know her, and heard her lively, impertinent, intelligent put-downs he was hooked and drawn to her … all of a sudden her eyes began to flash with great magnetic beauty! The mind transforms the body.

It happens the other way around, too. I saw pictures of a certain woman author who I thought was very attractive and when I heard her interviewed and heard her whiny view of life expressed in a very inelegant accent (from a small region of this land I shall not name) all of a sudden the next time I looked at a picture of her I thought she *looked* pitiful and mean. Same picture, but her looks had changed!

I loved also what you said about Mr. Bennet's humor. The critics thought that Mr. Bennet should have been more upset more often to show his compassion. Critics are often wrong, though.

For example, Rosemary Thornton (an author) wrote a review of one of my books in which she said, "Near page 150 (varies with different editions), the author [me] writes, 'raising your self-esteem is up to you. You can build self-esteem in a prison cell, in solitary confinement even. It does not depend on the thoughts or actions of other human beings.'"

She then says "I'd like to know the source for that info. Surveys done with women show that more than 3/4ths of women rely on a romantic partner to increase their self-esteem. Pulling one's self up by one's own bootstraps is more than a physical impossibility; it's also mighty tough if you've never heard good things about yourself."

Is Rosemary Thornton right about that? That three-fourths of women rely on a romantic partner for their self-esteem? Does Miranda rely on you for her self esteem?

Isn't self-esteem self-generated? Isn't that why they call it *self-esteem*? And how stupid would a woman have to be to rely on her romantic partner for her self-esteem? Isn't that Jane Austen's whole comedic point? Wasn't Elizabeth Bennet heroic because she was such a totally self-responsible, proudly independent person? Wasn't Darcy the same?

In my experience, women who rely on their partners for their self-esteem never have any. Because they are looking in the wrong place. Jane Austen would be a good place for Rosemary to start a remedial reading program.

Steve

29 December 2007 – Gilbert, Arizona
Dear Terry,

I got a handwritten letter in the mail from you today dated December 24, thanks! Your handwriting has not changed since I first met you in 1955! My handwriting changes almost by the hour. I've really got to learn to settle down.

Your opening sentence said, "Well, Merry Christmas or Season's Greetings if you're still subscribing to the newspaper." This reference will be obvious to the many, many scholars who've pored over our books. In a footnote to a future annotated version of *this* book they'll point out that in our last book, the one about obituaries, I ranted and raved about how our Phoenix newspaper had dropped its traditional MERRY CHRISTMAS wish in its December 25 headline and replaced it with the wussy "Season's Greetings." I fired off an angry letter in which I canceled my subscription.

Here's an update: they somehow never took my cancellation seriously because we continued to get the paper. Which was a good thing because Kathy likes to read certain sections and do the crossword. But even better: for each Christmas thereafter they have put up a huge red and green MERRY CHRISTMAS on the front page! I like to imagine that my letter sent transformative shockwaves through the newsroom.

Thanks for including with your letter the obituary of Laura Huxley from the *NYTimes*. She lived to be 96! You highlighted in yellow the part about her having written a self-help book, *You Are Not The Target*, in 1963. I actually read that book in the mid1960s! Way before I went into the profession of self-help, motivation or whatever it is now called. And although the *Times* (of course!) wanted to make the book look silly, ("The book offers a set of what Mrs. Huxley called recipes for getting through life's many difficulties. These include punching a tetherball, imagining one's own funeral and dancing in the nude,") I remember the book had a very positive, long-lasting impact on me. Especially in its central concept: You are not the target. I've used that idea ever since I read her book. I've also used it to help coaching clients who think they are unfairly targeted. When Darcy was haughty and dismissive of Elizabeth at the ball, it would have helped her to realize right then and there that she, Elizabeth, was not the target.

Have a safe journey to Mexico, especially that last trek through the mountains by mule to your home, Steve.

30Dec07 – NYC, NY

Steve,

I'm off to Mexico tomorrow, but I think there's little chance I'll subliminally tie *Mansfield Park* to the high Mexican desert as you suggest I'm in danger of doing. When I am reading Jane I am fully in her world – the English countryside at the turn of the 19th century. I almost never see one of my dark Mexican-Indian neighbors and think, "Wow, does Jose ever remind me of Darcy!" Just doesn't happen.

Terry.

1 January 2008 – Gilbert, Arizona

Terry,

Happy New Year!

And thanks also for sending me that little article about the mischief some people are committing inside bookstores. It said that some people are putting little religious tracts inside secular books, and others (people of the opposite persuasion) are moving bibles into the Science Fiction section! I'm sure you sent it to me because I have in the past suggested that you do a similar form of "reverse shoplifting" in the many book stores of New York.

Reverse shoplifting is something I have done a lot of in my earlier days as an author … when I was fearful and desperate … and what you do is this: you take a book of yours *into* a bookstore and put it in the shelf! Then you wander out, hoping they didn't see you do it. I used to do a lot of this pathetic trick. I'd wander into a bookstore with a book of mine in hand, and then pick the place I wanted it to be, say "New Arrivals," and I would then pretend to be reading the first few pages of my book, and then I'd slowly put my book into "New Arrivals" and pick another book up from that table and look at it in the same way, then slowly put that one back. Then, just to seal the deal, I'd go buy a book, wait in line and then pay and leave. Mission accomplished! The bookstore now has a copy of one of my books! Someone will pick it up and buy it, and it will be entered into the computer as a sale, and it might even trigger the system to order another! Soon you've got a word-of-mouth bestseller. Why do I call this system pathetic? Because it is. That's probably why you raised your eyebrows noncommitally when I urged you to do it with our first two books in New York. You know math and statistics better than I do. How many years would this really take to make a book a bestseller? A few thousand years? How old are we right now?

Upon reflecting on this article about people moving bibles into the Science Fiction shelves, it caused me to wonder where they would move books about Scientology? If they moved them to Science Fiction, L. Ron Hubbard would say – "Make my day!"

This reminds me of a similar bit of mischief I used to do as a boy. I'm not proud of this either, but I might as well do the whole confessional here. I used to go into greeting card shops and change some of the cards around. I would take a card from the Congratulations category and put it up first in the Sympathy category. So someone looking for a sympathy card would pull a card out that said, "Congratulations! You Deserve It!" People looking in the Wedding category would pull out a card that said, "We Share Your Grief. But This Too Shall Pass." When I told Kathy I used to do that her opinion of me went down another notch.

Hasta luego,
Steve.

January 1, 2008 – San Miguel de Allende, Mexico
Steve,

Happy New Year, yourself!

We got up early in the morning yesterday in New York in order to pack and do a few errands before catching a plane first to Atlanta and, from there, another to Leon, Mexico. From Leon there is a hair-raising, one-and-a-half-hour van ride through the inky Mexican night on a two-lane twisty road to get to our home here in San Miguel.

We arrived in time to celebrate New York City's New Year at 11 (after all, that's where we'd started the day) and then the Mexican New Year at midnight. It was a long day and it took a lot out of me. Approximately four seconds into the New Year I was asleep.

In general, I must say the flights were enjoyable because much of the time was spent reading the opening chapters of *Mansfield Park*. Once again I am thoroughly into a world created by Jane Austen. But doesn't this seem a much different world than the one in *Pride and Prejudice*? It feels somehow darker. While in *P&P* the antagonists were merely silly or stupid (sometimes both), here I sense they have the capacity for meanness or even evil.

I say that, and then am not so sure. Am I getting this feeling from Jane's words or from overlaying my impressions from the movie version of the novel which I just saw a couple of months ago? At any rate a very different feeling between the two novels would seem inevitable if only for the striking difference in the heroines. Fanny Price ain't no Elizabeth Bennet. On the other hand, who is? Also, to be fair, in *P&P* we meet Elizabeth at 20, whereas Fanny is only 10 or so when *Mansfield Park* begins and only 18 by the end of our assigned first seven chapters.

Naturally, however, there are many commonalities in the two novels. Most pleasing is Jane's wonderful sense of humor and sometimes-epigrammatic style, which I was glad to see again in evidence in these, opening chapters. Even as a more mature writer trying to write in a more naturalistic style, Jane cannot resist the polish and sparkle of lines like: "An engaged woman is always more agreeable than a disengaged," or "Selfishness must always be forgiven you know, because there is no hope for a cure."

I mean these could be lines from an Oscar Wilde play. In fact, reading them and especially reading chapter 5, I am struck by what a wonderful playwright Jane would have made.

Chapter 5 consists almost entirely of two separate conversations between various characters. The one is a discussion largely on marriage; the other concerns itself with delineating the fine points and boundary of a woman's being "out" or "not out." They are wonderful scenes because, while seemingly not advancing the story, in fact, through the players' expressions of their opinions and the style with which they do so, they very much reveal pieces of their character. The scenes would fit wonderfully, virtually verbatim, in the first act of a play on social manners.

I might add that the second conversation is especially helpful to 21st century readers because the concept of being "out" or "not out" doesn't exist today. Or rather the concept exists, but in an entirely different context.

One final thought on these chapters: Does it not strike you that Jane Austen has commandeered the plot of "Cinderella" for *Mansfield Park* with Mrs. Norris in the role of the wicked stepmother and Maria and Julia serving as the two doted-on older sisters? Of course there is the difference that Cinderella knew immediately on meeting the prince that she was in love, while, by the end of chapter 7, we have again the familiar Jane Austen heroine who the reader knows is in love, but who hasn't yet faced the realization herself.

Terry.

6 January 2008 – Gilbert, Arizona
dear Terry,

Glad you finally made it. I remember riding in the van along those winding mountain roads from Leon to San Miguel, but we did it in the daylight and the sights were captivating (goats, burros, abandoned cars, horse skeletons, wild dogs, great visuals). I sympathize with your travel fatigue, I have a hard time understanding, myself, why I can be so tired after just sitting on an airplane, but somehow all the processing through the airports, and maybe even having one's body hurled through the heavens at such speed is a bit of a drain. Imagine putting a gerbil into a model airplane and flying it all around the neighborhood for a half day. It would be tired afterward, wouldn't it? It would not want to stay up and celebrate with Dick Clark.

Your observation that Fanny in *Mansfield Park* is like Cinderella is really spot on! And not many writers can create such a tale that lures you in as if you've entered a very real-feeling yet other-worldly world of the author's creation. And yes, this one is darker and more complex than *P&P*. *Pride and Prejudice* was jubilant and comic, and the heroine, Elizabeth was bold and bright and hilarious in her scathing ironic humor. Fanny is the opposite of Elizabeth. And I am intrigued by Jane Austen's skill here in trying something so different. Challenging herself to write a novel so different. Almost like Dylan going electric, but this time it's in the opposite direction. From the electric Elizabeth she's transitioning to Fanny who is unplugged: a shy, self-sacrificing, self-effacing Fanny. Even more daring is that Fanny is self-pitying. Can you effectively create a self-pitying heroine? She's doing it so far. Your Mexican neighbors down there would call Fanny "Pobrecita!" Fanny cries a lot. Especially when thinking about herself.

She is adopted into a hostile and huge place, this *Mansfield Park*. And if it were not for the compassionate Edmund she'd have no one. But we see Edmund caring for her, giving her books to read like Henry Higgins did to improve Eliza Doolittle, and looking after her in wonderful ways. We're only seven chapters in, but it's clear that this is a book that is, as you say, dark. But dark in an intriguing way. Where is she going with all this?

You introduced me to this experience of reading for deep fantasy pleasure when we were both 11 and you strongly urged me to read the Oz books. Of course I knew the *Wizard of Oz* from the movie that frightened me as a child in the very same way that Hillary Clinton frightens me today … the witch and her flying monkeys were looked at in the theater between my fingers. You gave me the other Oz books by Frank L. Baum, like *The Road to Oz*, *Ozma of Oz*, and there were 14 of them! Amazing books to get lost in.

Prior to that, I'd never really been enchanted by reading. I didn't know it was possible. I'd been reading children's versions of great biographies of John Paul Jones, Daniel Boone, etc. but never anything like this where one leaves this world for another. Ever since then, I've been hooked, but the challenge is to find authors who can really take you there.

Entering the very grown-up fairy tale world of Jane Austen is a great pleasure, because it is both fairy-tale unreal and yet all about love and money and status and heartbreak and becoming a responsible adult interacting with society. All at once!

Getting lost in this fairy tale might be seen as escapism. But I see it as the opposite. I see it as traveling deep within, deeper still, down, down to your true potential.

Joseph Campbell's study of how mythology calls to the deepest part of us is very inspiring stuff. Campbell said, "I don't believe people are looking for the meaning of life as much as they are looking for the experience of being alive," and then he said, "If you follow your bliss, doors will open for you that wouldn't have opened for anyone else." My bliss was in those Oz books you pushed me to read.

In his complex and detailed masterpiece *Lectures on Literature*, Vladimir Nabokov in each chapter is addressing his lit students at Cornell. Prior to his chapter of lectures about *Mansfield Park* he tells his students how to be a good reader, and he says a great novel can only be truly appreciated when one is re-reading it, not in the initial reading. Then as he begins his chapter on *MP* he urges us to plunge "deep into the book and bathe in it, not wade through it." Well, I look back on what I did when we read *Moby-Dick* and I have to admit I waded through it. As fast as I could! Because it was so over-wrought and ponderous and Pynchon-like in its lack of poetic grace and charm. Now I'm thinking a re-reading would give me a better view? Maybe. But I'm not doing it.

For we are not serious students or critics of literature, are we? You and I? Aren't we just two guys reading Jane Austen? That's what the book says we are, and I'm sticking to that.

But still I've been thinking a lot about Nabokov's reprimand to re-read the great novels and to bathe in them and not wade through them. It would be almost a heroic act to do such a thing in this culture we live in today. To actually bathe in the re-reading of a great novel. Do you know anybody who does that? Who thinks they have the time?

When you read about Jane Austen's life, you think she can always retire to a quiet room in a large English estate and write. What's the distraction? Someone calling you to tea or whist every three hours? Those are three precious hours spent in nearly total silence. (Except for the ducks. Ever notice when you watch British movies or TV that there are always ducks quacking in the background? There must be a lot of ducks in England. But even so, they wouldn't distract you nearly so much as someone on a cell phone. Or a loud TV. Or even these days a car riding through the neighborhood with the big hip hop bass speakers pounding so loudly that one's windows rattle.)

Now I look back on an email I got from you today. The email says:

"My problem right now is that our internet is not hooked up at home yet)this also keeps us from Skype for the moment). I am instead at an internet cafe and it{s not ideal.)For instance, I don{t know how to do an apostrophe on the Mexican keyboard). Plus other obvious glitches, like where's the frontwards parens?"

What a world we live in! But as you told me in New York, Mexico affords you more peace and reflective time than NYC does.
Enjoy Mexico. s.

Jan 7, 2008 – San Miguel de Allende
Steve,
You may remember that I spent some time trying to decide between *Mansfield Park* and *Emma* as the second novel to read for this book. In the end I went with *Mansfield Park* because I remembered Vladimir Nabokov had picked it over the other Austen works for his famous Cornell University course in great literature. That was certainly recommendation enough for me.

I won't deny that I also figured that I'd be able to pick up some of Nabokov's insights on *MP* and pass them off as my own in our correspondence. You can imagine my chagrin on reading your last letter and finding you quoting from Nabokov's lectures as collected in *Lectures On Literature*.

Even more distressing was that when, after my last letter, I finally started reading Nabokov's lecture on *MP* the first thing that pops up is him saying that *MP* is clearly based on the "Cinderella" myth.

I honestly thought that had been my own discovery – that I had outed the source of Jane's plot. I do recognize, however, that I might have a hard time convincing you of that at this point.

A couple of other interesting things in *Lectures*: first that it was actually Edmund Wilson who recommended *Mansfield Park* to Nabokov. And second that Nabokov's favorite American authors were Hawthorne and *Melville*! We must have really missed something in *Moby-Dick*.

The Nabokov line you quoted about "bathing" in the book rather than "wading through" is philosophically what I believe is true of everything in life. The deeper you go into *any* subject, the more intellectually rewarding and enjoyable it becomes. This, I hasten to add, does not usually translate into *financial* reward. In fact, I believe the marketplace tends to value wide knowledge very much over depth.

I certainly don't resent this especially since I managed to parlay wide knowledge into a successful 30-year advertising career and scores of satisfying Trivial Pursuit triumphs. But now that money becomes less important to me, I long for more depth in the things I attend to. (I have always felt that money was essentially important to the extent that it could buy freedom. And now I seem to have all the freedom I can make use of.) I want to follow Nabokov's advice to "fondle and caress the details – the divine details."

I mentioned earlier the film of *Mansfield Park*. Now that I'm further into the book I feel I must warn you about this film. Not that the film's bad – in fact, I quite enjoyed it. It's just that it takes a number of liberties with the novel. The director has obviously borrowed real events and facts from Jane's life and given them to the film character of Fanny Price.

She (the director) has also injected a social consciousness into the film that I have not yet found anywhere in the book. This last involves the morally objectionable nature of the Bertram fortune, based, as it is, on the slave labor employed on the Antigua plantations.

The film I'm talking about is the 1999 version that features the playwright Harold Pinter in the role of Mr. Bertram. And no, I have no idea why the director felt she had to enhance the story of the novel. Why did she feel it necessary to improve on Jane?

And to end, I think I've told you about Miranda's and my annual Awards Dinner where the two of us name our choices for the previous year's "bests" in a variety of categories (best film, best meal, best play, etc.). For the first time in the 23 years we've been doing this, three of my top five books were *non*-fiction. Is this a sign of age? I read somewhere that as you get older you are less amused by fictions.

You will not be surprised, however, to hear that my Best Book winner for 2007 *was* a novel – *Pride and Prejudice*.

Terry.

10 Jan 2008 – Gilbert-AZ

Terry.

A recent email from you cheers the Michigan victory over Florida in football. And now Michigan has a new coach who is famous for high-scoring wide-open offenses. But tell me this. Does offense win football games? Or defense?

I've always thought this was a meaningless question, yet you hear coaches like Bo Schembechler say, "It's a fact, defense wins football games." But how could that be a fact? If you look at a game from the mathematical viewpoint, you can see that the winning comes from outscoring your opponent. How can you win a game 41-35 and say that defense wins football games? Offense wins football games *and* defense wins football games. Which do you believe wins more games?

I think Jane Austen believed it was both. Offense (Elizabeth Bennet) was fun and spirited and outgoing. And now Defense (Fanny Price) quiet, withdrawn, shy, contemplative, a Cinderella-type victim of psychological abuse, is also maybe even more of an intriguing winner.

So Jane Austen, being brighter than Bo Schembechler, is trying to say it's both.

Steve.

15 jan 2008 – San Miguel de Allende, GTO, MX
Steve,

I know that this has been a question that has been debated for years, but I *do* believe Jane would have made a great football coach. Not a blocking-and-tackling type, but a speed-and-deception coach. Her books are all about X's and O's.

The *Mansfield Park* young people in trying to find a suitable play to perform discard one after another for various reasons. But the objection I liked best was: "Not a tolerable woman's part in the play!" Does this sound familiar, and even current? Isn't it the same complaint you hear so often from today's actresses about film scripts?

I wonder if it's really true or if it's merely a convenient excuse that *sounds* as if it should be true? I suppose it must be actually true because otherwise talented actresses like Britney Spears and the various former Spice Girls would certainly have been in better films.

One thing it *does* explain is why there have been so many films made of Jane Austen novels – always loaded with good female roles.

The chapters we just finished in *Mansfield Park* (8 through 15) are almost entirely concerned with two smallish events in an English country neighborhood: the day's outing to Sotherton (estate of the proposed groom of Maria Bertram) and the planning of an amateur home theatrical performance.

This is where Jane is fabulous – in these unexceptional events in country life. If these things were described to you as major events in a novel, you'd make a special point of noting the title just to make sure you didn't pick it up by accident. And yet, Jane makes the incidents crackle with scheming and intrigue. As Nabokov points out, the Sotherton excursion is laid out like moves in a chess game. (Or, like X's and O's.)

What struck me is that both the outing and the theatrical scenes are all about pairings and unpairings and endless scheming to create pairings. There is, of course, one major theme recurring through all of these maneuverings: Fanny is always left alone. At Sotherton she is the third wheel to one pair of characters after another. And in the casting of the play, she is again the cast-aside, urged to take the role of the cottager's wife – a role usually thought of as fit for only a governess to play.

A few other thoughts on various characters:

Mr. Rushworth is certainly *Mansfield Park*'s Mr. Collins. Both outrageous buffoons, both endlessly concerned with the outward manifestations of their own status and place in society. Jane obviously has great fun with these characters, but might it be that they're a bit overdone?

The main difference between the characters of Elizabeth in *P&P* and Fanny in *MP*: Elizabeth is too sure of her opinions; Fanny too unsure. This certainly makes Elizabeth the more enjoyable character to read, but I don't think it makes Fanny any less valid. On the other hand, the thing I hate about Fanny is that she's so sickly and susceptible to drafts and exposure to the sun, etc. Get a few good meals in the girl; put some meat on her bones; and send her off to Outward Bound!

And then, of course, there's Edmund: sober-thinking, thoughtful, considerate, maybe just a wee bit too conservative Edmund. And yet! He is just as quick to throw all sense and reason to the winds for the sake of a pretty face as all the rest of us are.

How many times have you done that, Steve? Made a bad or wrong decision based on a woman's pretty face or pleasing form? I cannot begin to estimate my own count.

The irony is that it's women, of course, who have the reputation for losing their senses for love. And yet I rarely see women making these mistakes. It is always men who seem to play the fool. I would love to think that it's biology rather than stupidity. But sometimes I have my doubts.

Terry.

19 January 2007 – Gilbert, Arizona
dear Terry,

I've always thought that what you said at the end of that last letter is true. But no one realizes it. Everyone thinks it's women who are greater fools for love. But I, like you, think it's men.

Look at OJ. He thinks Nicole is seeing some young handsome guy and he dons a ninja outfit, swigs down some high grade cocaine, slips on some gloves and goes out into the night to teach her a lesson. All for love. Or the perception of lost love. Do women usually go that far? [*As the more cautious of the two authors, I must point out that Steve's OJ theory has not yet been proved. TNH*]

In our novel poor little Fanny is almost the opposite of Elizabeth Bennet as a heroine. She is sweet and still, like a martyr, like a saint like a clear pool of water. People are mean to her and take advantage of her. Cinderella! But she takes it all in and never wavers. Whereas Elizabeth was a great ball of fire. I remember the scene in *Pride and Prejudice* where Elizabeth sits down at the piano and captivates Darcy with her playing while disclaiming any great skill. She was like Jerry Lee Lewis in that scene. Jerry Lee wasn't Van Cliburn, but he had magic in his playing, and a kind of reckless bravado that we love. Goodness gracious great balls of fire.

Fanny, of course, plays no instrument.

And Fanny receives all kinds of nastiness from the other humans at Mansfield Park. Mrs. Norris is particularly nasty to her. Mrs. Norris is so nasty to Fanny that no one will ever forget it! For example, in the Harry Potter novels, Argus Filch, the caretaker at Hogwarts School, has a prying cat – loathed by all the students –

named "Mrs Norris," after the judgmental, busybody character in *Mansfield*.

The essayist Ellen Moody thought we readers all react personally to Mrs. Norris because we all know the same type of unhappy woman. Women who criticize and judge everyone else and are caricatures of pessimism. We all have one of those in the family. Ellen Moody asks, "Who has not met a Mrs Norris? Did you confront her? Probably not. You got out of the room. If she was your aunt and it was a family holiday, you sat far away. In Austen's time people had to spend all year with their family members, not just holiday."

This is a profound insight into why Jane Austen's novels are so good. I can't tell you how many people complain to me after a holiday gathering with their family how stressful it was. How upset they got with one of their parents, or a brother or sister. Or their sister in law. High psychodrama at these family gatherings. Even the spiritual sage Ram Dass used to say, "If you think you're enlightened, go spend some time with your family." That always got a huge, long-lasting laugh at one of Ram Dass's talks because everyone seemed to be able to concede that time with the family was a mixed blessing, a tossed mix of negative emotions. Suicide rates go up during Christmas vacation.

Now imagine that this Thanksgiving gathering has to last all year long! All life long! (That was country life in England.) Many people would just leave the room. But that's why the psychological mysteries and dramas in Jane Austen are so good. That's why she's been so popular for so long.

Some religions believe that when you die you are reunited with all your family members in heaven. Is that a positive reason for converting to this religion? (Further studies show that people in those religions have a greater fear of death than average people do.)

You mention how you are getting tired of how sickly and vulnerable our heroine little Fanny is. I think Jane Austen was trying something very daring with this book. Creating a heroine who was not heroic. I laughed when you said she should fatten up, get outdoors and go to Outward Bound! Outward Bound! "What is that?" I wondered. I mean I think I know by the sound of it that it must be one of those programs that builds your self-esteem through wilderness quests. So I looked it up and my guess was correct. But it's funny that you would know about this and I would not. Because I know you think I go too far with all this motivational stuff I do. But you have to understand that you walked a healthier path in life. While I was a mess. In fact, you might not even relate to people talking about how stressful their family memories are.

Self-help is made fun of by intellectuals in the *New York Times*, but it saved my life. However, I realize that I tend to take it too far. Not everyone wants to keep hearing about the latest program for enlightenment and motivation.

My own dear wife Kathy keeps me honest. When she catches me dispensing a little too much wisdom about the power of positive thinking at a family gathering, she will roll her eyes and say something funny about me. Which reminds me of a joke:

A woman is told by her doctor she has six months to live. "Is there anything I can do?" she asks.

"Yes there is," the doctor replies. "You could marry a motivational speaker."

"How will that help my illness?" the woman asks.

"Oh, it won't help your illness," says the doctor, "but it will make six months seem like an eternity."

s.

20jan08 – san miguel, MX
Steve,

The reason I *know* about Outward Bound is that I once was the writer for a Canadian television show that was basically about people who took risks. We did a segment on a girl who went to Outward Bound in British Columbia.

The reason you *don't* know about Outward Bound is that it all takes place in one of your least favorite places – The Great Outdoors.

Reading your comments on families made me realize how revered the concept is here in Mexico. While most of the United States worships at the altar of Work & Career, down here it's all about Family.

I have wondered if this is more a function of the Catholic Church's emphasis on family or of the fact that in Mexico's relatively undeveloped economy there are many fewer opportunities for fulfilling careers.

t.

22 January 2008 – Gilbert, Arizona
dear Terry,

When you said little frail Fanny should be fattened up and sent on an Outward Bound adventure, I wondered … how fat do you want her to be?

And immediately I (and right here we're going to see another example of 60's summer-of-love drug lingo now being used as everyday language) … and immediately I flashed back on being in a grocery store checkout line a few years ago, staring at a tabloid paper headline that said, "GARTH BROOKS LEAVES WIFE FOR TWO-HUNDRED-POUND WOMAN!" Somehow I have never been able to shake that headline from my mind. Of all the irrational things for a man to do.

But look at how times have changed. That headline ran a few years ago. That was when a 200-pound woman was considered to be bordering on being a circus freak. Today, for Garth to merit a fresh headline, he'd have to leave his current wife for someone who weighed a great deal more. (They say the universe is expanding. We live in exciting times.)

It's fun reading Nabokov's lecture on *Mansfield Park* right along with the book. Nabokov, in my opinion, was the greatest writer the English language ever saw. His joyful love of words is always contagious. Like when he points out in this lecture that the word "embargo" is "O grab me" spelled backwards.

Nabokov admired this book we are reading and said it was "the work of a lady and the game of a child. But from that workbasket comes exquisite needlework art, and there is a streak of marvelous genius in the child."

Jane Austen's needlework genius was hard for me to read at the beginning. But once I got into it, her weird compelling characters and stories within the stories kept drawing me forward, and now I don't want to stop reading. I know if I'd had to read this in college my attitude would be that it was merely hard work. I would have needed amphetamines to really get into it. (No, I wasn't sane in college, but you already knew that.) Hard books used to make me feel stupid. Henry James? Forget about it.

Speaking of stupid, Kathy sent me this blond joke today. In it the blond says: "Got really excited … finished jigsaw puzzle in 6 months … and the box said '2-4 years!'" And that's how I feel reading this great literature with you.

Tell me you are safe down there in Mexico. All the news reports I read these days focus on the drug cartels and the killings. But I remember the village you live in as being happy and peaceful. (Like *Mansfield Park* itself, far away from the wars and even the chaos of London.) I hope San Miguel de Allende stays that way. Because this just came across a news site, "Mexican Attorney General Eduardo Medina Mora told Mexican media that drug and organized crime related killings rose to 2,500 in 2007, up from 2,350 in 2006." I looked at those numbers for a while and then it hit me: 2,350 and then 2,500. The killers must be very organized and cold-blooded indeed to be able to control their death count to come out in such perfect round numbers. So be careful. If you hear that there have been 2,699 killings near the end of 2008 you might want to stay indoors.

love to Miranda, Steve

Jan 23, 2008 – Manzanillo, MX
Steve,

I believe we are safe here in Mexico because we have signed up with what I consider the strongest cartel. Naturally it would be foolhardy for us to join one of the weaker ones, and I am not foolhardy. So don't worry about us.

t.

Jan 23, 2008
T,

Tell me. How does one choose the ideal cartel?

s.

Jan 23, 2008 – Manzanillo, MX
Steve,

Good question. Many people make horrible mistakes joining cartels down here. Sure they live it up for a while, but eventually they have to pay the piper. This payment is usually made by getting blown up by a car bomb or gunned down on the street (*calle* we call it down here) by a bunch of guys in ski masks.

It's sad.

Especially when it could all be so easily avoided by doing just a little research before committing to a particular cartel. But what to look for?

I've long subscribed to what I call the Holy Cartel Trinity: 1) appearances, 2) connections, and 3) track record. This research can be done right at home in newspapers or on the internet.

Appearances. Search the web for pictures of top echelon members of your short-list cartels. Think former Panama strongman Manuel Noriega here: heavy-set, jowly, pockmarked, thuggish. Look for guys that look like that; none of the top-flight cartels have pretty-boy capos. The problem here is that most of these guys have been on the lam so long that the most recent photos are often ten years old. It's hard to tell what they look like now. Move on, then, to …

Connections. See how often the cartels honchos are linked to heads of state, other high-ranking politicians, members of the judiciary, A-list movie stars, etc. Don't forget to check the gossip columns. Often you'll find mention or a picture of some brand name capo knocking back a few margaritas with, say, Lindsay Lohan at some West Hollywood after-hours club. The problem here, of course, is that Lindsay ain't got no juice: she can't quash an indictment; she can't order a retaliatory hit; she can't even talk her way out of a speeding ticket. Move on to the third and most critical measure …

Track Record. Cartels don't publish annual reports or offer full disclosure on their sales figures or trends. This makes a financial evaluation mere guesswork. Not helpful. But what is readily available in the press is information about takedowns – assassinations. No, I grant you they don't publish daily standings like in the other major sports, but any competent newspaper reader can quickly put together a pretty fair approximation.

Reviewing these three facets will usually turn up a pretty obvious choice among the cartels. Hope this is helpful.

Terry.

24 January 2008 – Santa Monica, California
Hi Terry,

I'm here in Santa Monica in my hotel room getting ready to do some work with my friends at the University of Santa Monica. A copy of Jane Austen open on the bed, notes falling out of it, I wonder if she knew ... if she knew that people would be reading her after all these years.

So little Fanny is alone, a martyr, but growing stronger. She is principled, and knows what's honorable and right. While all around her the other characters act up and act out. Grown up children who cannot delay gratification. The social butterflies, the busybodies, the hollow sensualists, the pleasure-seekers and the aging adolescents whose arrested emotional development Jane Austen skewers with wit and irony and devastating sarcasm. These Crawfords and their like (and even Edmund is seduced by all this desperate, romantically needy energy) are grown children who have no reality unless they are socializing, posturing, story-telling and being bon vivants. The shallowest of people. We all know people like that. They don't really exist for themselves, except when they are impressing others. Alone Fanny holds out for honor and truth. The eye of the hurricane. The center of the fiery storm. Tom Wolfe called such a flagrant gathering of appetites a bonfire of the vanities.

When you and I were 20 years old a movie came out called *The Pleasure Seekers* with a dream cast of Ann-Margret, Tony Franciosa and Gardner McKay. Do you remember it? It was warning us. Where does such shallow pleasure-seeking lead? Yesterday the news was that the young actor Heath Ledger was dead. Empty pill bottles all over his apartment. Sleeping pills.

But sleep won't come. The whole night through. Your cheating heart. Will tell on you.

Because it's cheating to want inner peace to be so immediate and easy.

This I have to remind myself every day. Just like your own disciplines of writing and walking and journaling do. I use something I call The Stravinsky Code to remind me of where real joy (versus shallow gratification) comes from. It's a quote from the composer Igor Stravinsky. He said, (and I've read this a thousand times by now striving to have it sink in really deep), "My freedom will be so much the greater and more meaningful the more narrowly I limit my field of action and the more I surround myself with obstacles. Whatever diminishes constraint diminishes strength. The more constraints one imposes, the more one frees one's self of the chains that shackle the spirit."

Here's to obstacles,   s.

28 January 2008 – Santa Monica, California
hey Ter-bear,

(I'm borrowing your mom's favorite nickname for you so that it doesn't fade from the record.)

I know I'm weighing in early on this part of the book, but I just can't wait to write to you about it. I am still in my Santa Monica hotel room with rain and wind battering the window, a little lamp on the desk illuminating all my wildly-scribbled notes taken while reading Jane last night and earlier this morning.

In this part of our story, Fanny is blossoming into a beautiful woman. She has been well mentored by her cousin Edmund, whom she adores. And now the cocksure ladies' man Henry Crawford has decided to flirt with her. But not just flirt with her, but do something even nastier. Here is the cocky Crawford talking to his sister Mary:

"And how do you think I mean to amuse myself, Mary, on the days that I do not hunt? I have a plan for these intermediate days, and what do you think it is? My plan is to make Fanny Price in love with me."

When Mary tells him he is ridiculous, and that he should focus on Fanny's cousins whose hearts he has already toyed with, Henry

Crawford says, "But I cannot be satisfied without Fanny Price, without making a small hole in Fanny Price's heart."

(Rick Springfield, Wishbone Ash, Cyndi Lauper, and Kelley Willis are among the many singers who have songs called "Hole in My Heart." Cyndi Lauper sings, "I've got a hole in my heart that goes all the way to China." So hers is the saddest, I think, though none of them are very happy.)

Henry Crawford is, in the word popular in Jane Austen's era, a coxcomb, and my dictionary says that meant that he was "a vain, showy fellow; a conceited, silly man, fond of display." I remember fraternity guys in college like Henry Crawford. The word for him in college would have been "cocksman" which the *Urban Dictionary* defines as, "A male that is a user of women. Similar to a gigolo but does not necessarily rely on a monetary goal. For no other reason than conquests of women closely surrounding this person's life are his driving force."

Jane Austen really knows how to write about this kind of man. She was 20 when she wrote *Pride and Prejudice*, the sweeping, pulsing love story written by a brilliant 20-year-old mind. But *Mansfield Park* was written when she was 36, in those days a confirmed spinster, and actually just five years from her death. So this book was written by a deeper, wiser woman. Many people call it more somber, but I think it's more brilliant. In fact, I have to confess that I have raced ahead of our schedule in my reading because I can't help it. This book is so much more captivating than the first one you and I read. The complex kindnesses and cruelties performed by people in this book are mesmerizing. It's written by a writer at the very top of her game.

Jane's being 36 doesn't sound very old to us. (Because we all know that 36 is the new 16 today). But in Jane Austen's day 36 was time to really get down and tell it as it is … as if there were no tomorrow.

As we've been reading these two books, I have wondered what it is that makes Jane Austen so great. And I think Henry Crawford hit on it for me. When he says, up above, that walking and riding would exercise his body, but flirtation – and getting Fanny to fall in love with him – would exercise is mind. And that's it. Right there. Jane Austen is the absolute master at presenting love as a function of the mind. Because her modesty disallowed any overt sexuality in the books, she had to focus on the mind. A perfect thing to focus on in a book.

And I think the mind is the most neglected aspect of falling in love. Especially in books and films today! Today the author takes flirtation immediately into the bedroom. In *Atonement* the boy flirts with the girl then pins her to the library wall like a dead butterfly as both beings sweat, sprocket and gasp in pornographic ecstasy. It's just too quick and easy. All so quick, down and dirty today. Like that thoroughly modern play we saw together recently in New York, "Hoodoo Love": curtain rises on the two main characters copulating to the point of climax! There's very little intelligence required of the writer of that scene (although *Atonement* writer Ian McEwan has plenty of intelligence, he lacks Jane Austen's heart and certainly her soul.)

Jane Austen has her characters talk, question, flirt, debate, tease and confide with each other in glittering spirals of richly intelligent dialogue until I find myself just loving them. I almost love them all by the finish. These aren't cartoon characters; they are subtly layered in so many wonderful ways. Just like real people in our lives. I even can't wait for the obnoxious Mrs. Norris to reappear with her latest burst of psychopathology.

Henry Crawford's decision to get Fanny to fall for him as a form of his own amusement reminds me of a fascinating movie called *In The Company of Men*. Two junior executives on a long business trip, both of whom have been recently hurt by women, decide to get even with women for their past hurts: They intend to find, romance, and then dump a vulnerable woman.

The movie was howled at and hissed at by outraged critics who thought it went too far beyond good taste. But that was the movie's point. (If we can watch Hannibal Lecter without complaining, then we can watch these guys.) This movie wanted to explore the darkest side of the male ego.

In *In The Company of Men* Aaron Eckhardt (a wonderful actor, an ex-Mormon) and his pal plot an immoral strategy to get revenge on women. As if all women are any "woman." They plan to manipulate and seduce a sweet, innocent woman (like Henry plans to entice Fanny) and then dump her abruptly with her feelings and self-esteem completely destroyed. When they meet the deaf secretary Cristina (played by Stacy Edwards), they find their perfect victim. However, things get complicated when one of the men falls in love with Cristina.

Does this plot description sound familiar? Although the film was thought to be almost too edgy and out-of-the-box-evil even for modern times, it is a perfect mirror of Henry Crawford's plans with our dear, vulnerable Fanny. Which is just one of many reasons why Jane Austen is so widely read today.

Henry Crawford wants to put a hole in Fanny's heart that goes all the way to China. For his amusement. Will Fanny be able to resist? Stay tuned.

Hope you're enjoying Mexico. I was happy to get your message that you've chosen the right drug cartel to align with down there so that your lives will have a certain degree of protection. (Still, though. I'll feel better when you're back on the safe streets of New York. And I noticed when I was last down there with you in San Miguel that the streets there are cobbled. So be careful on your daily power walk that you don't incur a sprain.)

Steve

28 Jan. 2008
Santa Monica, California

let me ask you, TERRY,

Would you say that our dear little Fanny, who is called a "creepmouse" in the book by Tom Bertram, is in reality not a creepmouse? Would you even guess that she is (instead of being a mouse) a buxom, lusty, beaming big girl with tousled unruly blonde hair, huge energy, and quick infectious laughter? An irrepressible born-to-run filly? I would say not. I suspect you would say "hardly." And yet.

And yet that is how the PBS Masterpiece Theater production of Mansfield Park portrayed her last night! What were they thinking? That a creepmouse would not get ratings, is my guess. That if Fanny was the heroine, then we must make her more like the Bavarian milkmaid in a porn flick. (As I imagine she might be.) So people don't tune out.

Yet it is that very creepmouse that is Jane Austen's boldest creation as a writer. Fanny blossoms in the book, but slowly, and she never loses her shy humility.

In the TV version she was running everywhere, bosom heaving, bodice begging to be ripped, blonde curls tangled by the wind, huge and constant radiant smiles melting viewers' hearts. And by so doing, the whole brooding depth of the story was lost. I'm almost glad now that Jane Austen died at 41 so she couldn't see this stupidity played out. Did you see it?

Steve

1feb2008 –San Miguel de Allende, Mexico
Steve,

No, I didn't see it. We don't get Masterpiece Theater down here. But given your description, it doesn't sound as if I missed much.

These chapters (16-24) definitely could be called "The Blooming of Fanny Price." Suddenly everyone and her uncle's noticing her. Her uncle, after years of seeing her more or less as inoffensive wallpaper does a double take; Mrs. Grant starts inviting her to dinner; and Henry Crawford now wants her in his trophy case.

By the way, you liken Crawford to the Aaron Eckhardt character in *In The Company of Men* (a film I've not seen). What came to my mind when I read the Crawfords' conversation you

quoted was the Malkovich character in *Dangerous Liaisons*. God
what vain, self-centered and, I might say, cruel jerks men are. Or
can be anyway. Women can be hurtful too, of course, but I think
men take home the majority of the hardware at that particular
awards ceremony.

When I was at Michigan, there were fraternities (thank God not
mine!) that used to organize events called "Pig Parties." The idea
was that each member would get a date with the ugliest girl he
could find and then they'd all show up at the party. I can't
remember what was supposed to happen then; I think a variety of
demeaning incidents were planned. Can you think of anything more
gratuitously cruel? I cry at the recollection.

I mean imagine these girls, knowing, of course, that they were
not beauties, but suddenly a boy had invited them to a party.
Imagine how thrilled they must have been – and then when the
dreadful realization dawned, as inevitably it would at some point ...
well, there my imagination fails. How indescribably awful that
must have felt. As I said, I cry.

"The envelope, please ... and now, ladies and gentlemen, the
award for total lack of compassion, feeling and common decency
goes to ... well, no surprise here – Men!" I think there might be a
possible hint here as to why war is a primarily male pastime.

Obviously Henry Crawford isn't that depraved, but it's patent
which side of the line he's on.

One of the effects Jane's books have on me is regret. Her better
characters' standards of morality, kindness and manners make me
look back on some of the events in my life and feel pangs of sharp
disappointment with myself. Supposing the standards held by the
best of her characters were Jane's own, she makes me wish I could
somehow show her my life and be given her seal of approval. And
I feel I'd fall short in her eyes.

This is, naturally, beyond ridiculous and I feel vaguely foolish
even writing about these feelings, but they are nonetheless there.
Nor do I mean this as some kind of a major confession; because
the truth is that I see myself as basically a good, and occasionally
even admirable, person. I write that last without blushing, though

perhaps I should. It's just that reading Jane makes me wish I'd lived to a higher standard. (It's not as if I haven't had more immediate examples to follow. I've been married, as you know, to two women, each of whom I consider to be a much better person than I.)

Amazingly, Jane creates this feeling in me without ever seeming sententious, preachy or holier-than-thou. And I can think of no other writer who makes me feel this way, including (perhaps *especially* including) any number of far more overtly "moral" writers.

In the recent film *The Jane Austen Book Club*, there is a particularly hokey scene in which a character is about to cross the street on her way to making a bad moral choice and when she looks at the "walk/don't-walk" sign, it starts flashing the words "What would Jane Austen do?" Watching the film I thought it was by far the weakest moment in what was otherwise a very entertaining film. Reading what I've been writing, maybe it wasn't so hokey after all.

And, yes, I am resolved to be a better person from this moment forward.

t.

2 February 2008 – Gilbert, Arizona
Dear Terry,

Most people don't know when they're going to die. Jane Austen didn't know she was going to die at the age of 41.

Because I got swept up and cheated and raced ahead in *Mansfield Park* I put that book away and began reading *Becoming Jane Austen* by Jon Spence the biography the movie we both saw was based on. This is quite a life story, and I am so impressed with Jane Austen's quiet courage. She died in a brave, uncomplaining way from an illness. She was never very much of a whiner or a show horse in any way. She never even put her name on her books during her lifetime.

I contrast such devotion to one's art to so many of the people I meet today in business or the self-help field. People who rush to publish a book for the sole reason of having their name on it and putting their name "out there" like a virus in the world. They don't much care how good the book is.

Norman Mailer was an author who got so intoxicated by his own fame that he forgot to keep writing good books, with a few exceptions. Mailer died a few months ago, and just prior to that he used a funny metaphor to describe how one never knows when one will die: "You just don't know when the ball's going to roll off the table," he told an interviewer.

Virginia Woolf, one of Jane Austen's greatest fans, actually did know when the ball was going to roll off of her table, because she rolled it herself. Weighing her pockets down with ball-shaped stones she walked deep into a river near her home and drowned at the age of 59. We studied her book *Mrs. Dalloway* in college, and had I not been forced to read Virginia Woolf and George Eliot I think I would have not realized so early in life that as hard as it was for them to be taken seriously, there were great women writers all along.

Camille Paglia sounded a lot like you today when she wrote about Hillary Clinton, "But Hillary herself, with her thin, spotty record, tangled psychological baggage, and maundering blowhard of a husband, is also a mighty big roll of the dice. She is a brittle, relentless manipulator with few stable core values who shuffles through useful personalities like a card shark ("Cue the tears!"). Forget all her little gold crosses: Hillary's real god is political expediency. Do Americans truly want this hard-bitten Machiavellian back in the White House? Day one will just be more of the same."

I remember your fury when Hillary didn't answer your letters calling on her to explain her Iraq war vote. And speaking of fury ...

You once wrote a rather chilling short story that I really liked called, I think I remember this right, "The Divorce Club." In your story, like in Miss Austen's books, the intriguing characters were women, but not lively, heroic women like Elizabeth Bennet but rather more like Mary Crawford. Women who were bright but not as anchored. Like when Mary Crawford tries to talk Edmund out of becoming a clergyman. She rather flirtatiously mocks him for it, but he held his ground.

I don't always know who to cheer for in these moments. Just like the conflict I felt so deeply when the beautiful screen actress Dolores Hart, who starred opposite Elvis in *Loving You* and *King Creole*, left Hollywood shortly thereafter to become a nun! Many people admired her for that, but I was 19 when it happened, so I was more like Mary Crawford in thinking "My goodness what a waste!" Today I admire her. Today the Reverend Mother Dolores Hart is Prioress at an abbey in Connecticut. She chants in Latin eight times a day.

Whereas Elvis … well that ball rolled off the table a good while ago.

I am examining your latest letter containing your itinerary and I see that according to the schedule you ought to now be back from your sojourn into Mexico City and other even more exotic places. Yet I haven't heard a word from you since you sent me that message. I worry. Kathy and I have a close friend who had one of her relatives kidnapped in Mexico City not long ago, never to be found. I asked her how such a bizarre thing could have happened and she said it was not bizarre in Mexico City. She said kidnapping had become all too common a crime there. So I worry. I've not been contacted for ransom. But I have not heard from you, either. You have no Skype phone because your computer is missing some key electronic elements. You guys don't have your own cell phone either. Normally this is an admirable lifestyle choice not to be so available to the world. But when one's friend worries … still, no ransom demand. What would I be willing to pay, you are wondering. Everything. I'd liquidate it all. And that might be a reckless thing to say so publicly in a book, but criminals don't read. Which is one of the reasons they are criminals.

love to Miranda, or to her memory, whichever applies, until I hear from you

(meanwhile I am waiting like those guys with big radar discs who wait for contact from extraterrestrial beings after having sent into the cosmos an ill-chosen audio cocktail of Bill Haley music and Richard Nixon speeches)

s.

3FEB – SMA, MX
Steve,

Actually, I find that as much as I might agree with what Paglia said about Hillary, I can't say those things out loud without consequences. I get pegged as anti-female, or anti-Clinton (Bill). When, in fact, I think I'm neither. I am, however, opposed to politicians who glance at a Gallop Poll before casting a vote. Plus I was strongly against the war in Iraq. Hillary voted for it. Well, of course, so did Edwards, who I could have lived with. The difference is that Edwards has since acknowledged that vote as a mistake; Hillary still claims it was the right thing to do.

I can admire Hillary for her steadfastness and sticking up for what she believes I suppose. But at the same time I am also left to draw the inevitable conclusion that if she were President and were faced with *exactly* the same situation, she'd pull the trigger again. How can she possibly claim she wouldn't?

She must be thrilled that all the newspapers – and more importantly for her, the polls – are now saying that the war in Iraq has been supplanted as the voters' most important issue by the economy.

t.

5 February 2008 – Gilbert, Arizona

Dear Terry,

I love what you said about how Jane Austen causes you to reflect and evaluate your own moral history and principles in life. I have known you since you were 11 years old, and if you have anything to regret in how you've lived your life, I wouldn't know what it was. I was trying to think, but I couldn't come up with anything. Maybe you've covered it up like Nixon. But I doubt that.

Here's something I hold you in the highest esteem for: you have always brought good cheer, humor and happiness to everyone you encountered, and I don't mean just special people, but everyone. All the time. You are a light to people.

It started when you were young ... maybe as a schtick to get attention during those days when we so wanted to get noticed. You were hilarious. Always funny. I remember one time standing in the hall with you in junior high school when two pretty girls came up to us giggling and they said to you, "Say something funny, Terry! Be funny!"

And I thought to myself, oh no. The poor guy. How does one perform on demand like that?

And you weren't fazed at all ... in fact you pretended to be shocked and frightened by what they said, you made a grotesque face (and in this you were always like Jack Nicholson, never afraid of what your face looked like, willing to contort it any which way for a laugh while the rest of us were frozen in fear trying so hard to always just look cool) and you started backing away from them and me and you put your leg into a large trash can in the corner of the hallway and you began climbing into the can. It was one of the funniest things I ever saw and the two girls were laughing so hard it was more than they had bargained for.

And it never has stopped. Even when you and I walked the streets of San Miguel last year people who recognized you would always brighten when they saw you, "Terry!" they would cry out from across the street. And you would mumble to me that San Miguel was "like Mayberry" for the Americans down there. That it's basically a small town and everybody knows everybody. But when that person crossed the street to get to you, you were open and funny and always referring to something about that person that you had remembered from a previous conversation or encounter.

I have always been in awe of your unstoppable good cheer with other people. You make people laugh and feel great about themselves. Jane Austen would have been crazy about you.

I have wondered deeply about this because I am not nearly so gracious with people. Especially people I don't know too well. But you are happy with everyone. Waiters and taxi drivers, bellboys and fruit vendors. It doesn't matter to you. You light them up, like a night on Broadway.

When I wonder about your ability to do this, I wonder if it wasn't a subconscious mission you had to not inherit your father's painfully shy social demeanor. It's almost as if you went in the complete opposite direction. Not consciously, because you idolized him. But maybe you subconsciously decided that the shy approach would not be for you. The point here is that people always brighten up in your presence.

I'm almost the opposite. I'm a rather dark, haunted figure socially. (I always hate reading FBI profiles of serial killers, haunted, awkward, socially conflicted people … I'm afraid police are going to come knocking on my door.) People are always telling me how hard I am to get to know. How turned off they are when they first meet me. "You totally blew me off" my good friend Gil told me the other day recalling our first encounter at a birthday party. Another person I recently met called a mutual friend and said, "I was not at all impressed by Chandler. I met him on the elevator, and he's not exactly an inspiring person is he?" My friend said, "You have to get to know him."

Hey, so maybe I'm Darcy! (Positive spin. Maybe unmerited. Jane Austen originally called *Pride and Prejudice*, "First Impressions.")

But the point is that these things would never happen to you. You bring the light. If you don't mind me putting it in the lingo of my California friends, you bring the light. Everywhere you go. You bring full attention to everyone, you make everyone feel special, and you make everyone laugh. That's probably why you have no real interest in comedians or sitcoms. You already do what they do all day long. Their own efforts must look contrived.

But I'm not dismissing what you say. Jane Austen, especially in these two books, makes me see so clearly what a truly principled person is like, and how admirable, how admirable. What would Jane do? A great question, indeed. We have rented that movie but it won't be released on DVD until next week and I can't wait to see it.

Steve.

6feb2008 – San Miguel de Allende, Mexico
Steve,

I must say I am in total agreement with the sentiments expressed in your last letter. I am, without an iota of doubt, one pretty damned grand human being. I bring the light … and back-up batteries.

I do have to say though that I cannot remember during my entire three years in junior high *one* pretty girl – much less *two* – ever saying *anything* to me.

Terry.

7feb2008 – Gilbert, AZ
Terry,

Oh I remember that incident as if it were yesterday. I envied your comic instincts. Thanks for the memories … as Bob Hope used to sing, and thanks for recommending the movie, *The Jane Austen Book Club* …very entertaining romantic lighthearted fun and it really did focus on her books! Kathy and I saw it on DVD last night and it had a great bio of Jane Austen after the movie as one of the features ... one of the Austen scholars actually had the same Jane Austen action figure that I have in her office.

When my little grandson saw my action figure of Jane he was confused. (He has many action figures of his own, Spiderman and others too complicated to recount.) And he looked at the action figure and kept asking me, "What does she DO??" His action figures either shoot spider webs over their opponents, or turn the world to ice, or other things like that. Jane's just holds a quill. "What's that?" the eager six-year-old asked me pointing at her quill. "She writes with that," I said. He lost interest very quickly.

It seems to me that Jane turns the tables on who women really are. Her best characters are women. Her funniest and most principled characters are women. In *Mansfield Park* we almost think Edmund is the most principled and heroic character in there until Mary Crawford flirts him into playing a part in the play he morally objects to. That leaves Fanny as the final hero. The strongest person morally in the book. Jane's women are powerful.

This reverses the world-view held by most men. Most men I have met or read. Robert Graves said, "A woman is a muse or she is nothing." Jane Austen makes that incorrect.

Why read fiction? I know the answer when I am reading Jane Austen. Because there's more truth in it than in any other kind of book. In one of her diary entries Virginia Woolf writes, "The only exciting life is the imaginary one." And one agrees. Because one sees everyone on the airplane deeply engrossed in a book. Excited by what they are reading ... stories and characters imagined by the author.

These passengers could be talking to each other! Couldn't they? Some are, but that annoys everyone else trying to read. I no longer marvel at the huge headphones people wear that block out all sound and deliver white noise and silence to people reading something sprung from a novelist's or poet's imagination.

We are imagining reality anyway, aren't we? So many boring non-fiction books today are dull to read precisely because they are so unimaginative. But the minute you infuse some high imagination into a book, you've got something really worth reading, like the creatively written non-fiction of Michael Lewis or Tom Wolfe. Or Camille Paglia or Nora Ephron, or Joyce Carol Oates writing about boxing!

Einstein said, "Imagination is more important than knowledge," and he was one of the greatest scientists of all time.

Jane Austen was wittier than Dorothy Parker and a braver soul as well. Dorothy Parker attempted suicide five times. Her first book of poetry was called "Enough Rope." Finally she gave up on quick suicide and just increased her drinking in later life until she died of a heart attack at the age of 73. Her famous poem about suicide:

Razors pain you;
Rivers are damp;
Acids stain you;
and drugs cause cramp.
Guns aren't lawful;
Nooses give;
Gas smells awful;
You might as well live.

Give Miranda a hug for me and I hope you enjoyed watching your Giants win the Super Bowl this weekend … what a game it was!

Steve

Feb 6 (Chinese New Year's Eve) – San Miguel de Allende, MX

My favorite Dorothy Parker poem:

I like to have a Martini,
two at the very most;

three, I'm under the table,
four I'm under my host!

While certainly Dorothy made her reputation for saucy wit with her off-the-cuff comments and for oddball things like naming her parakeet Onan, because he "spilled his seed upon the ground," I gotta say the above poem gives her a lot of poet cred with me. Of course, it'll never be considered a great poem because it's too clever, in the same way Thurber or Wodehouse will never be considered great writers.

Did you ever see the film about Parker with Jennifer Jason Leigh? She really is one of my favorite actresses. Do NOT, however, see her latest film *Margot at the Wedding* – one of the most unrelentingly depressing films I've ever seen. I don't think Dorothy would be saying "might as well live" if she had seen this film. Leigh is very good in *Margot* but I kept asking myself "why would she do this film?" I found the answer about a month later: she's married to the director.

t.

7 Feb. 2008 – G Az

Ter,

Yes, Jennifer Jason Leigh was great in that Dorothy Parker movie ... *Mrs. Parker and the Vicious Circle*. She is quite a remarkable actress ... mesmerizing even. I recall you having seen her live on Broadway not too long ago and being almost shell-shocked at her allure. It was like I had to throw cold water on you to revive you. Wouldn't she have been a great Mary Crawford in Mansfield? Mary Crawford is like Elizabeth Bennet's evil twin – Elizabeth without the conscience.

Thanks for clarifying your Hillary Clinton position awhile back. She is not my candidate this election year; but I worry about mine. I may not be able to vote for my candidate, John McCain, because of his anger problem. It goes way back, too. Describing his own childhood, McCain has written: "At the smallest provocation I would go off into a mad frenzy, and then suddenly crash to the floor unconscious. When I got angry I held my breath until I blacked out."

Do we want his finger on the nuclear button?

S.

11 February 2008 – Gilbert AZ.

Dear Terry,

As a boy I idolized Prince Valiant, Superman, The Lone Ranger, and later Doak Walker (the football star) and then Norman Mailer, Dylan Thomas, Hunter Thompson (drunken writers I wanted to be like) and later the sober geniuses even more glorious like Vladimir Nabokov, Tom Wolfe, Emerson and Ken Wilber. All men all the time. But now so deep into Jane's brilliance, and Byron Katie's and Brenda Ueland's I have finally embraced the creativity these women teach. Total, thorough creativity. Divine writing.

Too often I have been one of those men Brenda Ueland described, ignorant about the role creativity plays in linking humans to the divine. Men like me.

"They do not know," Ueland writes, "as William Blake did, that not creating is a fearful sin against themselves. They would be much greater now, more full of light and power, if they had really written the sonnets and played the fiddle and wept over the sunset, as they wanted to."

And you have found the key to accessing that spirit. Just do it for an hour. Your method for ensuring creativity in each day reminds me of Lennon and McCartney's method for writing songs. They were asked how they did it. How was such magic produced? Their formula was finally revealed by them: "There are two things we always do when we sit down and write a song. First we sit down. Then we write a song."

People think it has to be more than that, so they don't do it.

Even the focus necessary to *read* is hard won. You can't even read in airports very easily because airports think we would rather have TVs blaring from every wall. It's Orwellian to have every human in the airport listening to Wolf Blitzer interpret the news. It used to be that our thoughts were private and separate. So I have to fight for that space today. That sense of clearing. The philosopher Heidegger used the concept of a "clearing," as a clearing in a forest (Lichtung), as the space inside consciousness where Being revealed itself. Without creating such a clearing for oneself, all the beauty of life would remain concealed by clutter and static and gossip.

Jane Austen creates a clearing within that clearing.

s.

12 feb 2008 – San Miguel de Allende, GTO, MX
Steve,

I feel inadequate to comment on the Brenda Ueland stuff you cite. I've read her book on writing and didn't find it compelling. I am afraid Fate dealt me an incomplete hand: I was unfortunately born without the spirituality gene of which Brenda was blessed with a lifetime supply. I simply find it hard to believe in anything I can't see or somehow prove. (This, of course, had also gotten me in hot water with God and his committed delegates.)

In today's world, this lacking is a huge handicap. I am constantly being told that some personal problem or complaint would be resolved if I would only get in touch with some puissant spirit residing within me. I always feel it pretty shabby of the spirit to take up residence within me and not introduce himself.

I am sure you're reading this and thinking that I am merely being superior. I am not. I honestly wish I could buy into these things – that I had the genius of belief. But I simply don't, and I suspect I never will. Fact is, I always feel vaguely embarrassed when someone starts telling me of the wonderful powers of some inner spirit. Or of the soul. Or of God. Perhaps when I grow older I'll have some deathbed conversion to the unbelievable. And as in the end of *Brideshead*, I'll acquire faith. But I'm sure not there yet.

The point of this? I think Jane's with me on all this. God is not really a character in her novels. Clergymen, certainly; but God? MIA. She presents the clergy as a social class rather than as representatives of a higher power. Some members of this class are charitable, useful and kind (Edmund Bertram) while others are silly, pompous and self-centered (Mr. Collins in P&P); but none seem particularly devout. I must say I like them better that way.

t.

14 February 2008 – Gilbert, Arizona
Dear Terry,

Wow. You were born without the spirituality gene? You know I wouldn't agree with that. But we must be talking semantics at this stage. So I'll respond to you this way. Not with my words, but with Dylan's from his song *Forever Young* (which I hope you stay.) May you grow up to be righteous / May you grow up to be true / May you always know the truth / And see the light surrounding you.

Kathy and I were driving home today after a Valentine's Day lunch here in town and she was reading to me from the local Gilbert newspaper as I drove. She read aloud the story of a town activist who was leading a recall drive against our mayor. The two men had confronted each other outside the Gilbert Civic Center recently and the mayor shouted at the activist, Fred Phyllis, saying, "You don't have the guts to run against me! You're a rotten piece of (expletive deleted) like you've always been!" Whereupon Fred Phyllis said to our mayor, "Go take your medication."

Prior to her reading me this wonderful story about our local politics, we had been discussing a possible move to Scottsdale. But upon hearing this I pointed out to Kathy that if we did move, we'd miss things like this. And she agreed that living in Scottsdale might be comparatively dull. We'd also miss the strong smell of horse manure each morning as we go outdoors to get the paper (Gilbert has a ton of "horse properties") and the sound of donkeys and roosters that greet the dawn. If we lived in Scottsdale. And we would miss the sound of the mayor! Braying before his medication.

s.

15 feb 2008 – San Miguel, MX
Steve,

Have you noticed that in his lecture on *Mansfield Park*, Nabokov pretty much just retells the story – but along the way he points out the skills Austen is using in managing the novel, in turning the story into a work of art. The things he points out are fairly mundane like structural devices, the scaffolding of her themes, etc. And the revelations are rarely startling. But they do show us the pattern of bricks and mortar behind the plaster façade of the novel as we read it. More than anything, they reveal the virtuosity of the mason.

One of the particular techniques she uses that Nabokov did *not* remark is her use of "things." She often uses these objects to bring out various aspects of her characters. Their thoughts, attitudes, feelings and beliefs – especially the ingrained ones that they'd never actually verbalize or perhaps aren't even truly aware of – often get revealed to us as reactions to "things."

I was kind of surprised Nabokov *didn't* point it out because, from the evidence of his notes, he was certainly aware of it. Look at the little drawings he did of carriages in the facsimile pages of his notes, for instance. And the carriages are a good example of what I'm talking about.

Every time carriage or transportation arrangements are mentioned, Austen tells us with specificity what kind of carriage or what the seating arrangements are. Each means of travel carried a small world of associations and significances. Of course, many of these are lost to today's readers in our carriageless world, but they're there nonetheless. And I think we still pick up a lot of the overtones of these associations in the characters' reactions to the "things."

In explaining the central idea behind Imagist poetry, William Carlos Williams famously wrote, "No ideas but in things." Jane Austen anticipates him by a century and a half. A horse is just a horse; but look how much we learn about the various characters' attitudes regarding Fanny's place in the world based on Austen's handling of all the discussions and maneuverings surrounding which horse Fanny would ride.

Or look at the significance of the East Room: Fanny gets to use it primarily because it's no longer being used as a schoolroom. Like the horse, the East Room isn't really hers, but it's available to her *if no one else wants it*. In these two "things," then, Jane skillfully shows us Fanny's second tier, hand-me down status in the Bertram family circle.

The book is loaded with "things" and their significances. There's Mary Crawford's harp. And in the section we just read (chapters 25-33), we have the extended incident of the necklace. A simple inanimate object, but in the drama and feelings that surround it, we have the essential conflicts of the entire novel.

Turning to Fanny's new Babe status, I must say that from a purely personal viewpoint I am glad Fanny has just come to bloom at the age of 18. I find I almost never like a woman who was beautiful when she was a girl. For if they are beautiful in their early teens, they are almost invariably ruined for life. They develop the attitude of the Beauty and it stays with them the rest of their lives

I know this is harsh and there are no doubt exceptions to this hypothesis, I simply haven't come across one yet. I also know that it is not totally the beautiful girl's fault, that it has a lot to do with the way people around them treat her and the expectations this treatment engenders in the Beauty. She grows up expecting and getting things that girls who are 15% less good-looking never will get. And would certainly never expect.

(I realize I have mis-written: it is not a question of whether the girl was *actually* beautiful or not when she was a young teen, but rather whether she *thought* she was beautiful. It is the thinking so that warps.)

I find it amazing how this disease so modifies the beautiful woman's mind that she carries the symptoms long after the cause has departed. Meaning I have met women grown puffy and triple-chinned in their sixties who still expect the prerogatives they were able to command when they were 16 when their very appearance stopped hearts and made eloquent men tongue-tied. Grotesquely these now slovenly women still bat their eyes and flirt.

I stand second to no man in lining up to praise the beautiful woman – but please let the knowledge of her beauty come when she is 18 or 20 and not when she is 13. I wonder what Blanche Albert's doing these days?

terry.

17 February 2008 – Tucson, Arizona
Dear Terry,

We are in Tucson for a gathering at the comedian Fred Knipe's house for a night of singing. Kathy and I have been learning a lot of new songs, including a lovely duet by Bing Crosby and Grace Kelly. More on that in a minute ...

I am fascinated by your theory that a beautiful girl becomes an unattractive woman ... and, as with most observations about women I defer to you. You have been a scholar over the years, but I believe I have found the one exception: Natalie Wood. She was amazingly beautiful as a girl (see her movies as a child actress on up to her final films) and equally beautiful as a woman until her death by accidental drowning at the age of 43.

And as to your cryptic allusion to one Blanche Albert – I do remember the name, but I can't picture her. Was she in junior high with us? (You've always had a better memory than I. I've always envied your total recall.) I know Leigh Young was in junior high with us, but I didn't consider her to be extremely beautiful back then. Rather attractive, in a fresh but plain way. However as a woman she blossomed and became Leigh Taylor-Young, the actress. Kathy and I saw her last year at a fundraising dinner in Los Angeles and even though she is our age (early sixties!) she is still very beautiful.

As far as our Fanny goes, she's been growing throughout this novel. She's become more physically attractive (otherwise shallow Henry Crawford would not have chosen to capture her heart for the sport of it) and under the tutelage of Edmund, her mind has grown as well. She quotes lines of great poetry here and there, whereas the other women in the story are not nearly so deep or cultured.

(In commenting on Fanny's education Nabokov contrasted her reading of poetry to the young women of his teaching days in the 1970s who were more into women's magazines for reading. Imagine if Nabokov could see today's young women hungrily scrolling through text messages on their iPhones as their primary reading. I read an article last week that revealed that high school graduates in the 1960s had over twice the vocabulary of young people today. The ratio was an average word-utility of 25,000 in the '60s to 10,000 words today!)

Now that we've read through Chapter 33 in *Mansfield Park* we've found that Henry Crawford has had a subtle change of heart. After deciding to get poor, gentle, shy Fanny to fall in love with him for the fun of it, he is rather astonished that she turns him away. That startles him and increases his interest in her. He now thinks he is in love. What has excited Henry Crawford the most is Fanny's inner strength. Because on the surface she is delicate and demure. But underneath she is power itself. (That's what makes Jane Austen so great and so endearing. Like that moment you pointed out in the movie *The Jane Austen Book Club* when the teacher is about to cross the street to have an affair with her student. And the sign says first DON'T WALK then WALK then it says WHAT WOULD JANE DO? Because Jane is all about principle. Living true to your highest ideals, your highest self. So after a heartbeat the electronic crossing sign says DON'T WALK, and the teacher turns away, leaves her handsome sexy young student standing by his motorcycle in despair, and she returns to her husband.)

Fanny has been turning handsome, wealthy Henry Crawford away. Because he is revolting to her for having seduced the married Maria Bertram. Or as the book puts it, "Fanny told him that she did not love him, could not love him, was sure she never should love him, that such a change was quite impossible; that the subject was most painful to her; that she must entreat him never to mention it again, to allow her to leave him at once, and let it be considered as concluded for ever."

This kind of ironclad certitude is how Jane Austen makes her heroines heroic. Because she shows us there is a beauty to morality. That it's not just a grim and guilty obligation. There's beauty in integrity! It's Jane's message if she has a message.

There's something more beautiful about Bing Crosby and Grace Kelly singing "True Love" than the country gal snarling about cheating. Or the song you played me in New York recently by Amy Winehouse about her refusing to go to rehab. We hate to admit it that the Grace Kelly song is better because we may look uncool. But isn't the story of Paul Newman and Joanne Woodward more beautiful than the story of Angelina Jolie dumping Billy Bob Thornton for a fling with Brad Pitt?

For a while Billy Bob was wearing a vial of Angelina's blood around his neck. He was so impressed that she had left someone else for him! And that vial didn't help the beauty of that story much. With me anyway. When I think about it. Can you picture yourself going into the Yale Club with a vial of Miranda's blood around your neck?

Jane Austen is the poet of the courage of faithful, true love. She is our guardian angel on high with nothing to do. But to give to me, and to give to you … love forever true.

You made a great point about the "things" in Mansfield Park that carry so much poetic weight and strength ... I will add the necklace she wears to the ball to your list. Funny that Nabokov's lectures don't single them out. He even wrote a book about how much history and meaning something as simple as a pencil can carry. He called his book *Transparent Things*.

The French poet Charles Peguy said, "It will never be known what acts of cowardice have been motivated by the fear of not looking sufficiently progressive."

So it may be hard to fault today's young people for not wanting their reading to be more than phone texts and e-mail. People today have to fight for silence and solitude. I have clients that I assign books to, but they "don't have time to read," even though the book, if carefully read, would solve everything.

I have clients who would solve their problems if they would just take a day off and sit alone in silence. But they won't do that, even though the great philosopher Blaise Pascal said, "All men's problems come from their inability to sit alone in a room for any length of time." Notice he said, "all" men's problems, not just "some" big problems. Even the smaller ones! My clients don't want to take their marching orders from Blaise Pascal. Darn it. I wish they did. It would make my job as a consultant so much easier.

They would rather hop in their car and crank up a song by the underground rapper Blaze Ya Dead Homie. (He records, by the way, on the Psychopathic Records label, and I am willing to bet your nephew Chato could tell us more about him, as he has schooled us in Kanye West recently. Psychopathic Records is an independent record label based in Royal Oak, Michigan, which was formed in 1991. Alex Abbiss and Horrorcore group Insane Clown Posse whose first successful release on that label was, "Carnival of Carnage." I only bring this up because "Carnival of Carnage" was said to be Jane Austen's working title for *Mansfield Park* until she made the title switch at the last minute prior to publication.)

But my noise-addicted client (I'll call him Rod) doesn't want to devote a day to silence because he is afraid. He fears not looking progressive. He fears not looking busy (to the people he fears.) Who are these people we all fear so much? Why do their opinions of us mean so much?

Rod shudders with horror at the concept of sitting in a chair in a quiet room all day with no contact with anyone. "I have to have constant contact with people," he says. "Or else they will lose faith in me."

So Rod races through life firing off emails and chattering on his cell phone. He communicates roughly 500 times a day. And his life is slipping away. It is being ushered out on the noise.

But this solitude – the silence – that we can go to for sustenance, can be terrifying when you think of it. But only when you think of it. So don't think of it in advance of it. Just go into it. Because I have found that when you actually go there it's reassuring. It lifts you up like a surfer's wave. Like a feather pillow. Like a night in the forest. Like a John Denver song. Like a sleepy blue ocean. Your senses fill up. They don't stress out and panic like you think they would.

So imagine now the courage of Jane Austen! Alone in her room for hours and hours writing her novels. And *what* novels. Were they ego boosters to make her more famous and appreciated? She couldn't even put her name on them. Her first novel was published with the author named only as "A Lady." That's it! Then back into her room to write another. Into the silence.

At around the age of 12, Thomas Edison started to lose his hearing. He was involuntarily ushered into a world that had more silence than other people had.

Amazingly Edison actually liked being deaf (technically, he was extremely hard of hearing, but not completely deaf). He said that it made it easier for him to concentrate on his experiments.

I remember being at your place in San Miguel and meeting your gardener and your housekeeper. These services are so inexpensive there that you can't not do it. Everyone wins. Except for one little thing. You said it makes it hard for you to write with them knocking about. You have to get out and go to a cafe somewhere. Were you Edison, you could sit right through everything writing to me about Jane Austen barely noticing them or anyone else.

Who was Blanche Albert?   S.

18 feb 2008 – San Miguel de Allende, MX.
Steve,

I know you were distracted by being at Fred's but please read my last letter again. I *did* mention the necklace in my discussion of Jane's freighting objects with significance.

And I *never* said that pretty girls become unattractive women. In fact I'd be willing to bet that the most reliable predictor of whether a girl will grow to be a pretty woman is whether she is pretty as a girl. What I *am* saying is that the beautiful woman who knew she was beautiful when she was thirteen will still be a not very nice person. She will expect to be catered to and have her whims treated as commands. And she will lack, what I call, a feeling for the ugly.

On the other hand the awkward, shy girl who blossoms into a beauty at 20 will never forget what it was like to be an outsider and how much it could hurt. She'll still feel for the girl that gets teased for wearing thick glasses or for the boy who is the last selected for the pick-up baseball game no matter how much she now gets per hour on the runway.

Blanche Albert was the Beauty of our class at Derby Junior High. She went "steady" with Lee Driver. After junior high, she went to a different high school than we did so we totally lost track of her.

And I don't know what you were looking at when we were at Derby, but you totally missed the boat on Leigh Young. She was heartbreakingly pretty; however, I think it took her a while to figure that out. She was in my "bloc" class and sat next to me three hours a day – very soft-spoken and shy. I remember she used to cover her mouth with her hand when she laughed; this self-consciousness is generally the mark of a girl who either used to wear braces or is Japanese.

I wrote the entire first draft of my first novel – the mystery story that was (probably properly) never published – while sitting in noisy cafes in Paris. That was my discipline there, I'd go to a café in the early afternoon, have two or three espressos or Diet Cokes and work on the book for a couple of hours. At the end I'd reward myself by ordering a glass of red wine and reading over what I'd written, maybe doing some light editing.

This would seem to contradict the traditional belief in the writer's need for solitude. But actually it doesn't. My French was so bad that I was never distracted by any of the conversations around me – they were all just white noise to me. And even though my Spanish is much better than my French ever was, I find much the same here when I go to a Mexican café down here. (I suppose it's the equivalent of Edison's deafness.)

I can't do this "blocking out" when I'm in New York. And I find busy bars and cafes there good for only reading or jotting notes. On the other hand, I will seek out unpopular places in which I'm the only customer; in these I can write. The problem, of course, is that these places tend to go out of business. That's what happens to places that have no customers.

t.

29 feb 2008 (Leap Day!) – San Miguel de Allende, MX
Steve,

These *Mansfield Park* chapters (34-41) are almost entirely concerned with Henry Crawford's pursuit of Fanny. And various stratagems are in play to effect her capitulation to Henry's obvious (to every character in the book but Fanny) charms.

Sir Thomas, wishing Fanny to see Henry as a "model of constancy," decides that the best way of creating this result "would be by not trying him too long." Accordingly, he makes an effort to put the pair together before Henry is to leave Mansfield Park. No go – Fanny is the Queen of Rebuff.

Next, Sir Thomas hits on the idea of sending Fanny back to her family for a long visit. Ostensibly done as a kindness to her, in fact Sir Thomas believes that a stiff dose of the coarseness and relative squalor of the Price family milieu in Portsmouth will make her more clearly see the benefits of a substantial income – the kind of income she'd have if she accepted Henry's proposal.

At this point Henry himself pulls off a rather brilliant move in the Fanny campaign. He suddenly appears in Portsmouth. Knowing a lot more about women than you do, let me assure you this is the kind of gesture women really fall for.

And yet, Fanny is a rock.

I'll bet she's beginning to find it rather frustrating that despite her blunt and unwavering assurances to all concerned that Henry is *not* the man for her – not now, not ever – no one seems to take her at her word. They all blithely assume that Henry with all his charm and lavish attentions will eventually win if not Fanny's heart, at least her hand.

That's basically the tenor and the direction of these chapters. So here's what I find so brilliant about Jane Austen: In the midst of all of Henry's earnestly pressing his suit, who does Jane give the most perceptive and prophetic line of dialogue to? Not Fanny. Not Edmund. No she hands the most important line in these chapters to the least perceptive character in the book – Lady Bertram.

You, Steve, must get the same feeling I do about Lady Bertram, that she hasn't a clue what's going on with any of the other people around her, that she's perpetually lost in the haze of her own indolence. And yet, who is it but Lady Bertram, who, after hearing Henry read from Shakespeare, says:

"You have a great turn for acting, I'm sure, Mr. Crawford."

This is, of course, the essential truth that no one else (except Fanny) seems to understand. So here's Lady Bertram wandering through the novel in a trance and yet it is she who unwittingly bumps into what everyone else is looking straight at but doesn't see.

I marvel at how perfect it was of Jane to put this line in Lady Bertram's mouth. If she'd had Sir Thomas or Edmund say it, we, the readers, would have paid too much attention to it and freighted it with significance.

In one of the Austen biographies I read, there was a description by one of her relatives of Jane sitting in family gatherings at home and occasionally a secret smile would come over her face. Then, sometimes chuckling to herself, she'd walk over to her writing table where she'd jot down a line or two or just make a quick note. And then she'd go back to her seat and rejoin the family conversation. I'll bet she had a very big private smile when she thought up that "acting" line and had the idea of having Lady Bertram deliver it.

There is also the subtle irony of Crawford's reading being from *Henry VIII*. Which is, of course, not only about a man named Henry but also a man who has more or less become the world prototype for a womanizer who constantly moves from one to another.

Before signing off, I'd like to kiss Jane's hem once more for her handling of another "thing." The silver knife, the object of contention between Susan and Betsey Price, becomes a small window for all of us to see Fanny's kindness, generosity and just plain good sense. "No ideas but in things."

But honestly, don't you find Fanny just a bit of a Goody Two-Shoes? Give me Lizzy Bennet's recklessly headlong misjudgments over Fanny's prissy perfection any day. It's like nobody goes to see *Gone With the Wind* and falls in love with Melanie.

Terry.

3 March 2008 – Vancouver Canada

Terry,

I'm here in Vancouver for a week delivering seminars, and while I was able to get your latest submission via the hotel computer, I'm now typing this out from hand-written notes strewn about my hotel room.

You're right! Lady Bertram's line is great. And wonderful coming from her. Until now, she's only been a rather lazy lump on the sofa with her little pug. For her to say that Henry is good at acting was subtly brilliant, and you got it and I missed it.

I have talked to you about this before. You are a patient reader. Doing what Nabokov recommends, bathing in the subtleties of a book. You've recommended books to me in the past that I lost patience with, even though I knew they were good. And I bet I would never have read any Jane Austen without you and Miranda and Kathy urging it. Again, the patience factor. But once I let myself patiently get into the rhythm of Austen's prose, I was hooked. (Amazing what we can do when we "have to.")

William F. Buckley's spy hero Blackford Oakes once said to another character, "By the way, Sally, does anybody ever confess to just plain 'reading' Jane Austen? I know only people who 'reread' Jane Austen." The Blackford Oakes spy thrillers are for impatient readers like me who enjoy high intellect but don't want to get into too deep a tub.

Do I think Fanny is a Goody Two-Shoes? I had to think about that. Then I decided to look that phrase up. Goody Two-Shoes is a fable from the 1700s – a variation of the Cinderella story. The fable told of a poor orphan girl named Margery Meanwell, who goes through life with only one shoe. When she is given a complete pair by a rich gentleman, she is so happy, that she tells everyone that she has "two shoes." Later, Margery becomes a teacher, and marries a rich widower. This earning of wealth serves as proof that her virtuousness has been rewarded, a popular theme in children's literature of the era. (And later, in Jane Austen's novels.)

I remembered, too, that Adam Ant had a great song called "Goody Two-Shoes" and lo and behold here it is on YouTube! Fun video too. Watch it and tell me what you think. He sings, "Goody Goody Two-Shoes, don't drink. don't smoke ... what DO you do? Subtle innuendoes follow, there must be something inside.." Great song, great rhythm and energy.

Is Fanny this? Yes I agree with you she is. But not in a shallow way. Because there are subtle innuendos and there is always something deeper inside her that grows throughout this book. When Henry Crawford asks Fanny for advice she tells him, "We have all a better guide in ourselves, if we would listen to it, than any other person can be."

Amazing how often the name Jane Austen comes up these days. Reading the paper this week about the Democratic primary race in Texas between Hillary Clinton and Barack Obama, I note that Maureen Dowd of the *NYTImes* writes, "At first in Austin, Hillary did not channel Jane Austen. She tried once more to cast Obama as a weak sister on his willingness to talk to Raúl Castro."

So maybe Obama is defeating Hillary because he is more like Jane Austen than she is. What a country! I do love it.

Fanny is sent to Portsmouth to spend a couple months with her biological parents. Her father is gross. He smells of alcohol and prefers reading the newspaper to talking to his daughter. He uses foul language.

Fanny is made uncomfortable by the lack of refinement in the home of her biological origin. It is rowdy and chaotic there. Fanny has come from the elegant and civilized Mansfield Park into Animal House. If John Belushi had existed back then, Austen would have put him in this house. These are very funny scenes Jane Austen creates and one can feel the enjoyment she takes in creating something so hilariously rowdy, smelly and chaotic.

love to Miranda and all your friends in Mexico ... I'll be seeing you two in New York soon. S.

4 March 2008 – SMA, MX
Steve,

I thank you for looking up Goody Two-Shoes because I was wondering about its origins myself. It was at first just a passing curiosity when I wrote the phrase but it became more acute when, the very next day, my Spanish teacher down here called me a Goody Two-Shoes when I bragged about how much I'd studied the night before.

(Seriously, Steve, how bizarre is that? In the first place Goody Two-Shoes isn't an epithet you hear all that often; then to run into it twice (!) in two days... And in the second place, my Spanish teacher, Riccardo, does not exactly have an encyclopedic knowledge of English. So how weird that among the relatively few English expressions at his disposal, one of them would be "Goody Two-Shoes [?!] ...)

Anyway, your little research clarified things for me. I mean I could understand the "Goody" part; but where, I wondered, did "Two-Shoes" come from?

So why didn't I just do the research myself? I haven't really explained this, Steve, but I am operating under a severe computer handicap down here. Our laptop is in its final days and is incredibly slow; there's something definitely wrong with it. It makes even the simplest internet searches painful experiences. Please let this explanation also serve as my backhand excuse for not being able to comment on Adam Ant's YouTube version of "Goody Two-Shoes." There is no possible way of seeing it on my laptop.

Maureen Dowd's Jane Austen reference about Hillary in Texas baffled me a bit. It seemed awfully strained. Didn't it to you? Could it possibly be that Maureen is under the impression that the capital of Texas was named after the English Belle of belles-lettres? She ought to do a quick check on the difference in spellings.

But even if Austin, Texas, *were* named after Jane, what point was she trying to make here? That Jane Austen had such good manners that she would have happily sat down to tea and conversation with Raoul Castro?!

I know, I know ... that is the second time in this letter I've used an exclamation point paired with a question mark. I admit it seems excessive, but after reviewing the instances, I stand by both as well warranted.

terry.

6 March 2008 – Santa Monica, California
Okay Terry ...

I'm in the lobby of a hotel in Santa Monica writing this. I'm writing it as fast as I can longhand, and later it will be typed into the book. There is a woman here, in the lobby, exposing her privates.

No, not her genital area. Not even her breasts. Worse. She is exposing something far more obscene and vulgar – her private conversations. Her innermost feelings!

She's on her cell phone.

And loudly spilling the mess of a shared life all over all of us. In a valley girl accent ... except that this is not a girl, it's a grown woman. And not a woman like the Jane Austen heroines who are so selective about who they share their confidences with.

No, this woman talking so loudly in this lobby is not an Austen woman. She is a woman whose life is an open wound. One guy is at his laptop computer, fighting to refocus on it as her life sprays all over him. Like a blood "spatter" pattern in a *CSI* show. Another elderly lady is reading her newspaper or at least trying to. And I have *Mansfield Park* opened in front of me but every time I try to find the passage I want this woman's horrible life invades my space.

According to what she loudly proclaims for all of us in the lobby to hear, she is misunderstood. She is being unfairly judged.

She has so many feelings. She says (to everyone in the lobby): "That's just the way I feel. I don't know. I could be wrong."

Why would a decent person not take her cell phone outside? Or into another room? Maybe this is just the collective unconscious Jung said we all shared really being shared.

No boundaries for this woman. Her desperate life spills all over the place. I am reminded of the scene in Leonard Cohen's novel *Beautiful Losers* when St. Katherine Tekakwitha spills a little wine on the tablecloth and the purple stain spreads and spreads until everyone and everything is purple. It keeps spreading until even the moon and stars turn purple from just one spill.

This is quite a spill we are hearing today. Quite a purple mess. Privates! These are her privates. Private feelings and opinions. They are for everyone.

What is she thinking? Making her conversation so loud and unavoidable to hear? Is this a cry for help? Will we all want to help her now? Once we all realize that she's misunderstood? Oh, lord, please don't let her be misunderstood. We could stage a "group" after she hangs up. I could lead it. Move the chairs in the lobby into a circle. Everyone talks. She could share further. We would give her feedback and loving support. Couldn't she just ask for that?

I'll tell you what separates this vulgar woman from an Austen heroine like Fanny in *Mansfield Park*. The internal component. So vital to a good life. This woman is never going to know about her inner wisdom. Not with that seductive, erotic toy she uses all day, her vibrating cell phone. ("Does the ringing bother you? I'll put it on VIBRATE!")

Oh, here's the passage I was searching for in Jane Austen.

When Henry Crawford asks Fanny for advice she tells him, "We have all a better guide in ourselves, if we would attend to it, than any other person can be."

Fanny's ability to turn to her inner guide is what distinguishes her from the rest of the people in this story. It's what makes her heroic. The men in the book are all fools. Edmund is the best of them. But still an absolute fool for not seeing the character defects in Mary and Henry Crawford – the defects that Fanny cannot just go along with. For love or for money.

What if we could put Fanny's words on every cell phone? We all have a better guide in ourselves than that shoulder you are about to cry on. If we would attend to it, better than any other person can be.

I wish I could finish by saying this: I took the cell phone from her hand, threw it in the koi pond, and handed her my heavily marked up copy of *Mansfield Park*. She took it and began reading immediately. Her life was never the same.

Steve

7 marzo 2008 – san miguel de allende, mexico
Steve,

It is, of course, fitting that your friend in the lobby would be exposing herself in Santa Monica. This otherwise pleasant seaside city has become pretty much the adopted capital of the Public Confession Movement (PCM) that has so swept the nation in our lifetime.

The manifestations of this Movement leave me feeling not so much invaded by the invariably shopworn emotions and opinions so openly spouted by the confessors; no, rather I am overcome by acute embarrassment. I don't resent these confessors, rather I die of mortification *for* them.

Por ejemplo (as they say down here):

As you know, San Miguel has a sizeable population of ex-pat Americans and Canadians. They've been largely recruited from three main groups: 1) older, retired people, 2) artists and wanna-be artists, and 3) adventurous people who are willing to pack up their lives and friends in Fargo or Des Moines and move to a new country, learn a new language and divide all prices by 10 to find out how many dollars they're paying for something.

I'm not sure how much you're up on human nature, but I'll give you a little lesson free of charge here. Each one of these three classifications of people contains an unusually high percentage of wackos. In the instance of the many San Miguel residents who fall into *all three* categories … well, that's called the "Wacko Triangle," and is considered *prima facie* evidence of extreme eccentricity, to put the condition politely.

I am giving you all of this valuable information with the full knowledge I may be damning myself. After all, a liberal interpretation of the categories might allow you to conclude that I myself am lost in the Wacko Triangle.

Anyway, that's all background to set the stage for a literary reading Miranda and I attended the other night. Now one might think that because the average age of the audience at this event probably started with a 7, that the traditional virtues of an earlier generation would prevail, that personal discretion and reserve would be the order of the day. One *might* think that if one neglected to consider the aforementioned wacko factor and the sweeping power of the Personal Confession Movement.

The reading was by a woman named Minerva Neiditz who wrote a book called: *Romance After 60: What Men Think They Want*. Well right away that should help define the audience. And yes, women were definitely in the majority. But what were all these *men* doing there? Because there were quite a few of us. Were we there because we really didn't know what we wanted? Were we hoping that a woman named Minerva (which classically suggests wisdom) would be able to tell us? Or maybe there just ain't that much to do on a Friday night at the old folks' home.

Actually the reading itself was fine. Minerva's bright and a good storyteller and her reading was quite entertaining. But at the end of this she put forward the thought that all of us were either "spiraling up" or "spiraling down" in life.

This struck me as a questionable premise. I mean can't someone just spiral in place? Or how about not "spiraling" at all? – you know, just kind of being stationary.

Let it pass, I told myself, and in a minute or two I'll be able to spiral on out of here.

Minerva had other ideas. Suddenly she was out there exhorting the crowd to share their spiraling experiences. "Are you spiraling up? Or down? Let's hear from you!" She reminded me of one of those Southern Baptist preachers asking his congregation if they were "ready to testify?"

Well – I was thinking – that was a pretty risky thing for a speaker to do. I mean what if no one spoke up? It seemed possible – after all I certainly wasn't about to. But Minerva obviously understood the power of the Personal Confession Movement better than I; for while I was still mulling over the question of whether I was spiraling at all or whether it was rather the effect of the tequila, members of the audience were already rising to testify. And damned if every single one of them wasn't spiraling *up*!

I found the whole thing incredibly embarrassing. It wasn't just because of the way these people were openly laying out their personal lives and tawdry "spiraling" epiphanies for the general examination – and presumed benefit – of the audience. But also because, even putting aside for a moment the semantic question of whether "spiral" is the right verb to describe my movement through the universe, I was still not sure if up or down was the correct direction. This was embarrassing in the face of the unanimity of the unwavering *up*sters in the crowd.

For a split second of insanity I was tempted to grab the floor and flood it with downward spiraling testimony:

"I am so spiraling down that people invite me to dinner parties when they don't have a corkscrew …

"I am so down that yesterday I spent an hour and a half stuck to the gum on the bottom of someone's shoe …

"I have so spiraled down that Exxon has me on retainer. They list me on their oil exploration budget …"

I did not, however, hijack the event, of course. Who wants to be a wet blanket in a throng of happily upward spiraling septuagenarians? Why do people do this? – spill their private lives out on the table for all to see? It's ego I think. I think these people actually believe that we want to know all about them. And, yes, I, like you, would prefer a society at least slightly more on the Jane Austen end of the spectrum than the Jerry Springer side.

As we walked out, Miranda commented that she didn't think either one of us would do well at an AA meeting.

～⚬⚬⚬～

Now comes a really interesting question, one that every writer faces. Obviously we all use actual experiences in our lives and people we know in some of the things we write. We can, of course, to some extent, disguise events and characters, but sometimes they're simply too obvious.

So should I leave this last story (and the opinions that went with it) in our book? For one thing, there will surely be a reading of this book in San Miguel after it comes out. There will probably be people in our audience that were in the *Romance After 60* audience.

Peter Mayle, who wrote *A Year in Provence*, had to move from the French town he wrote about because there was so much local resentment about what he'd written. Now if you've read his book, you'll know that he didn't really say anything all that damning about the place or the people – certainly nothing as bad as what I just wrote.

What do you think? For now I'm just going to let it ride, but there will come a time when I'll have to decide.

Terry.

8 March 2008 – Gilbert AZ
Terry,

Fanny talks about listening to the wisest counsel of all – your inner guide. But what if you are like Henry Crawford or John McCain and you have no inner guide? What do you listen to then? When John Kerry asked McCain if he'd consider being his VP McCain did not say no. Why? There was no inner guide. He didn't even know which party he should belong to. All he knew was that he liked being on television. So he met with Kerry to discuss it.

I don't pretend to know what went on in that meeting. How could I know? But I can guess pretty accurately. McCain said, "If I'm your vice president would I get to be on television a lot?"

"Yes. But a lot of it may involve explaining why you would run on a Democratic ticket after being a lifelong Republican."

McCain then was worried that this might be negative television. So he declined. There was never a consideration of the principles of the Democratic Party or the Republican Party. Because without an inner guide, you never have to bother with principles.

In a Jane Austen book John McCain would have been a character that we howled at.

Steve

16 March 2008 – Gilbert, Arizona
Terry,

In the last chapters of this book it feels as if our author has run out of energy. Everything winds down. And unlike the exciting flirtatious passions of Darcy and Elizabeth, we see Edmund getting over Mary Crawford and waking up, serenely, to the idea that he might want to marry Fanny, deciding to persuade her that her "warm and sisterly regard for him would be foundation enough for wedded love."

Would you yourself settle for a warm and sisterly marriage? That would be better than a rageful, destructive "Who's Afraid of Virginia Woolf" marriage, I guess. But I'd hope for a bit better.

But, sad to say, we are finished with *Mansfield Park*. A more mature and philosophical book, this one, and not one I would thrust into someone's hands and say "you must read this immediately!" Unless that person were on a desert island and could relax into it at the deepest levels of patient immersion. More like the way you read ... my bedroom and attention deficit office, on the other hand, are strewn with 20 to 30 half-finished books, all opened and ready to be picked up again. Impatiently I move from book to book, finding the right one in any given moment to suit my mood and current IQ level. (Yes, it varies. Wildly. Ask Kathy, who often has to dumb herself down to make communication possible. As I am reading a book about the life of Bo Schembechler.)

Austen winds this book down at the end in true Cinderella style by simply telling us that Fanny and Edmund lived happily ever after. No real dialogue or love scene between them. So the ending reads like an author's plot outline instead of the real ending. Maybe she had that outline handy and decided, "I'll just go with these notes as the end of the book. It's not like these books have my name on them or anything."

In a way I finally felt what you did about Fanny being Goody Two Shoes – she found her other shoe, oh goody. The goody-goodies win and the sexy Crawfords, Mary and Henry, lose. So the fire just goes out at the end and principle wins over pleasure-seeking. Mary in her saucy way tries to flirt and taunt Edmund out of being a minister, and Henry tries to seduce Fanny with his actor's charm. But they fail. I feel guilty for almost wanting them to succeed.

Emerson's words read at Frank Lloyd Wright's funeral were "Whoso would be a man, must be a nonconformist. Nothing is at last sacred but the integrity of your own mind."

For me, that sums up Jane Austen's heroines. True. Strong inside. Not conforming. Like Wyatt Earp as played by Kurt Russell in the great movie *Tombstone*. We watched that movie mesmerized the other night! It occurred to me that Jane Austen would have loved Wyatt Earp. (By the way, please do not just half read this paragraph and mistakenly rent Kevin Costner's *Wyatt Earp*.)

Jane Austen allows male readers a secret look into the minds of brilliant, creative, virtuous women. One heroine (Elizabeth Bennet) outgoing, another (Fanny) introspective. But Austen's heroines are each true to themselves and win in the end. Classy women who combine high intelligence with inner strength and virtue.

There is, on display quite often today, the opposite of a Jane Austen heroine. The angry and vulgar woman who blames her own lack of virtue on others. Who rants this way, as Erica Jong recently did, saying how tired she was of "pink" (blushing white) men. "I am so tired of pink men expecting that someone – a brown black yellow or white woman – will trail behind them changing light bulbs, taking out garbage, washing laundry, keeping God in the house, taking care of kids of all ages, of parents of all ages."

Do our women do that? Who is she talking about? (Where is her pharmacist?) I raised four children on my own for a long stretch of years.

This kind of victimized emotional ranting would not suit the great Austen women. This, although presented as acerbic and bitingly accurate gender comment – is actually more like sobbing, shrieking cheerleader beating on the chest pads of the football captain with clenched, inflamed (and pink) fists.

Jane Austen, on the other hand, works the high road. And even says to us, directly, in the last chapter of Mansfield Park, "Let other pens dwell on guilt and misery. I quit such odious subjects as soon as I can."

I am looking forward to seeing you and Miranda in a couple weeks in New York. Of course, I'm just assuming Miranda and Kathy will be with us … that they will not have grown tired of their pink men by then.

Steve

March 27, 2008 – Mexico City, Mexico (on the way back to NYC)
Steve,

Could I just start by saying I don't think of myself as a "pink man." After three months here in the Mexican sun, I see myself as more of a russet man.

Edmund wants "a warm and sisterly marriage?!" Maybe Jane *didn't* know that much about men. If she only could have heard Ohio State football coach Woody Hayes describing a tie in a football game as "like kissing your sister," she might not have described Edmund's desires in those words.

Jane here makes the mistake many women make. Despite overwhelming evidence to the contrary, most women honestly believe that men really want what women want. Then they get upset when we don't actually seem to.

I don't deny that there is some overlap in what the two sexes want, but it's far from an exact match.

Why *does* Jane run out of steam at the end of the book? Some of it may have to do with her natural inclination away from sentiment. While she's clearly in favor of feelings in the abstract, she tends to shy from the overtly sentimental on the page. Maybe it embarrasses her.

I have been reading the annotated version of *P&P* again while finishing *Mansfield Park* and I reached the endings of the two novels within a day of each other. One of the footnotes to *P&P* said that in almost all of Jane's books the climactic lovers' declarations scene is merely explained. We hear about it, but we don't actually see it happen.

Well, that certainly was the case in *Mansfield Park* in which we're told that Edmund and Fanny eventually get together but the revelation is virtually a codicil to the novel. But was it also true in *Pride and Prejudice*? I thought not, but in re-reading it I discovered that Jane, in fact led us right up to the moment of avowals and then retreated into a dispassionate summary paragraph.

I can fully understand Austen's reluctance to gush, but I do think the reader gets a little cheated. It's odd because it's not as if Jane can't handle emotionally charged scenes – witness Darcy's first proposal or Elizabeth's meeting with Lady Catharine at Longbourn.

In the movies of Jane's books, of course, all these scenes are fully played out on the screen. No director would ever allow Elizabeth and Darcy, or even Fanny and Edmund, to come to an understanding off camera.

It's interesting that these chapters (42-48) make up the end of the novel and yet rather than the focus being on Fanny and

Edmund, it is almost entirely on the Crawfords. And left to their own devices, those Crawfords show their true colors. Henry shamelessly runs off with Maria merely to satisfy his own ego; Mary simply reveals herself as the selfish bitch she is.

The Crawfords disintegrate before our eyes, while all we get on Fanny and Edmund's finding true love together is a single elegant but cool sentence: "… when it was quite natural that it should be so, and not a week earlier, Edmund did cease to care about Miss Crawford, and became anxious to marry Fanny."

Well … certainly no one can accuse Jane of getting sappy on us.

One last stunning thought struck me while reading a footnote from the *Annotated P&P*. The footnote commented on the silly Lydia using the word "fun" several times in one of her blabbering monologues. "Fun," the footnote pointed out, was still considered very much a slang word at the time and none of the ladies of quality in the novel (Elizabeth, Jane, Bingley's sisters, etc.) ever use the word at all.

This, of course, shows the excellence of Jane's craftsmanship. How she reveals character not just through *what* Lydia says, but even in *the way* she says it, the words she uses.

Of course, modern readers are so used to "fun" being an ordinary everyday word that we'd entirely miss the significance of Lydia's using it without the aid of the footnote. But here's my question, how many other period-specific clues like this lie in the text never to be discovered by us simply because we're reading her 200 years after the fact?

So the stunning thought was this: as much as we've admired Jane's brilliance as a writer – how much are we missing? The point is Jane is an even *more* brilliant writer than we can realize. And that, I think, should be the final word.

Terry.

About the Authors

Steve Chandler and Terrence N. Hill have been writers all their lives. This book is the third in a series that began with the critically acclaimed *Two Guys Read Moby Dick*, followed by the popular *Two Guys Read the Obituaries*.

Chandler has written and co-written over a dozen books, including the bestseller, *Fearless*. He is a professional business coach and corporate trainer whose previous books have been translated into over 20 languages. His blog, iMindShift, is popular around the world, and you can subscribe at his website, www.stevechandler.com. He lives with his wife and editor Kathy on the scenic outskirts of Phoenix in an old house overlooking Vista Allegre Park.

Terrence Hill worked for more than 30 years in advertising beginning as a copywriter and later running agencies in New York and Europe. He has published poetry, essays and short fiction and was the writer for two CBC-TV (Canada) documentary series. In 2005, Terry's play *Hamlet–The Sequel*, won the Playhouse on the Green (Bridgeport, Connecticut) playwriting competition. You can email Terry at terrynhill@hotmail.com.

ROBERT D. REED PUBLISHERS ORDER FORM

Call in your order for fast service and quantity discounts

(541) 347- 9882

OR order on-line at www.rdrpublishers.com using PayPal.

OR order by mail: Make a copy of this form; enclose payment information:

Robert D. Reed Publishers
1380 Face Rock Drive, Bandon, OR 97411

Note: Shipping is $3.50 1st book + $1 for each additional book.

Send indicated books to:

Name _____

Address _____

City _____State _____Zip _____

Phone _____Fax_____Cell _____

E-Mail _____

Payment by check /__/ or credit card /__/ *(All major credit cards are accepted.)*

Name on card _____

Card Number _____

Exp. Date _____Last 3-Digit number on back of card _____

Qty.

Two Guys Read Jane Austen
by Steve Chandler & Terrence N. Hill . . . . $11.95 _____

Two Guys Read Moby-Dick
by Steve Chandler & Terrence N. Hill . . . . $9.95 _____

Two Guys Read the Obituaries
by Steve Chandler & Terrence N. Hill . . . . $14.95 _____

Fearless
by Steve Chandler . . . . $12.95 _____

The Joy of Selling
by Steve Chandler. . . . . $11.95 _____

100 Ways to Create Wealth
by Steve Chandler & Sam Beckford . . . . $24.95 _____

Ten Commitments to Your Success
by Steve Chandler. . . . . $11.95 _____

Other book title(s) from www.rdrpublishers.com:

_____ $ _____

_____ $ _____